Table of Contents

Chapter 1
Introduction

Welcome to *The Independent Guide to Universal Studios Hollywood 2016*. This travel guide will take you through the entire process of visiting the theme park from choosing a hotel, to a look at each attraction, and even ways to save time in queue lines.

Universal Studios Hollywood (often abbreviated to USH herein) is the ninth most popular theme park in the USA, with almost 7 million visitors in 2014. However, comparing it to other theme parks is a bit unfair – USH is not just a theme park but a real working film studio going back over 100 years.

Even since opening day in 1915, the studio offered tours of the sets and backlots. In 1930, however, when movies with sound came about, the tour had to be discontinued as guests were disrupting production.

In 1964, the theme park experience opened with a revamped Studio Tour. Ever since, attractions have been added, the Studio Tour has been expanded and the park attracts more visitors than ever before. In total, the theme park now houses twenty attractions, shows and other experiences.

2016 is an extremely exciting time to visit as the park is going through a huge revamp with many new attractions. The Wizarding World of Harry Potter opened in April this year, with an incredible level of theming, live shows and fantastic rides. In Summer 2016, a new Walking Dead maze will also debut.

So, let's get into it!

Contact us

If you have any questions about your visit please contact us via the contact form on our website at **www.independentguidebooks.com**. Be sure to subscribe to our newsletter on the right hand side of the website for updates.

Limit of Liability and Disclaimer of Warranty

The publisher has used its best efforts in preparing this book, and the information provided herein is provided "as is." Independent Guides and the author make no representation or warranties with respect to the accuracy or completeness of the contents of this book and specifically disclaims any implied warranties of merchantability or fitness for any particular purpose and shall in no event be liable for any injury, loss of profit or any other commercial damage, including but not limited to special, incidental, consequential, or other damages. Please read all signs before entering attractions, as well as the terms and conditions of any companies' services that you use. Food prices are approximate, and do fluctuate.

COPYRIGHT NOTICE

Chapter 2

Tickets:

Getting the right Universal Studios Hollywood ticket is crucial, and it can save you a lot of money. There are several different ticket options to consider.

Advanced Tickets

Advanced tickets can be bought by guests from anywhere around the world. The easiest place to purchase these tickets is the official Universal Studios Hollywood website at **www.universalstudioshollywood.com**. There are two types of advanced tickets: General admission tickets that allow you access to the theme park on a pre-specified date, and Anytime tickets that allow you to enter the park any day, without having to choose the day in advance.

Child prices apply to children aged 3 to 9 years old. Children under 3 get free admission into the theme parks (proof of age may be requested on entry).

General Admission:

	Low Season	**Mid Season**	**High Season**	**Peak Season**
Adult	$90	$95	$100	$105
Child	$84	$89	$94	$99

Anytime Admission:

These tickets are priced at $115 per adult and $109 per child.

By visiting the Universal Studios Hollywood website and simulating a ticket purchase, you can check which price bracket your tickets will fall into. Advanced purchase general admission tickets are always $10 to $25 cheaper than tickets bought on the day itself at the theme park.

Front of the Line Ticket

A front of the line ticket allows access to the theme park for one day, and front of the line access to each attraction once, as well as priority seating at each show. Pricing is the same for each guest aged over 3.

	Low Season	**Mid Season**	**High Season**	**Peak Season**
Adult	$179	$199 to $209	$219 to $229	$239

Tickets bought on the Universal Studios Hollywood website will have a $0.99 fee added per ticket. In addition, tickets bought via the USH website include free Early Admission to the *The Wizarding World of Harry Potter*.

Advanced tickets are non-transferable, non-refundable and non-exchangeable. Tickets bought online can be printed at home, collected at kiosks at the entrance to the theme park, or shipped for an extra fee.

Gate Price Tickets

If you do not purchase your tickets in advance, you will need to purchase them at the theme park entrance ticket booths. These are "gate price" tickets, and essentially the same as anytime admission tickets featured above. They are priced at $115 for an adult and $109 for a child.

Front of the the Line tickets purchase at the theme park are $10 more expensive than the advanced purchase price.

Annual Passes

Annual passes allow you to visit Universal Studios Hollywood as often as you wish (subject to blackout dates on some passes) at a low per-visit price. In addition, special perks are offered to Passholders including discounts on dining and merchandise. There are three types of annual pass available.

	2016 Season Pass	Gold Annual Pass	Platinum Annual Pass
Pricing	$119	$299	$599
A year of unlimited admission	No. Entry 102 days per year.	No. Entry 313 days per year.	Yes. Entry 365 days per year.
Free parking	No	No	Yes
Discounted theme park and HHN tickets	Yes	Yes	Yes
One Free Halloween Horror Nights Ticket (select dates	No	No	Yes
Invitations to Annual Pass preview events	No	Yes	Yes
Discounted food, merchandise and specialty items	No	Yes (15%)	Yes (15%)
10-20% off certain CityWalk locations	Yes	Yes	Yes
Priority Boarding at Studio Tour	No	No	Yes

For the Season Pass, the first visit must be before 27th May and the pass expires 15th December 2016. All other annual passes are valid for one year.

Prices are the same for all guests regardless of age. A $10 discount is available for all passes bought online, except the Season Pass.

Top Tip: If you are planning two visits to the park within a period of 365 days, an annual pass can be a real bargain if the blackout dates work for you.

California Resident Annual Passes

	CA Resident Annual Pass	**CA Resident Plus Annual Pass**
Pricing	$149	$209
A year of unlimited admission	No. Entry 170 days per year.	No. Entry 246 days per year.
Free parking	No	No
Discounted theme park and HHN tickets	Yes	Yes
One Free Halloween Horror Nights Ticket (select dates)	No	No
Invitations to Annual Pass preview events	Yes	Yes
Discounted food, merchandise and specialty items	No	Yes (10%)
10-20% off certain CityWalk locations	Yes	Yes
Priority Boarding at Studio Tour	No	No

Annual Pass Blackout Dates:
2016 Season Pass:
Every Saturday and Sunday, plus:
May 2016 – 27th and 30th
June 2016 – 3rd, 10th, 13th to 30th
July 2016 – All month
August 2016 – 1st to 22nd
September 2016 – 2nd, 5th and 6th
October 2016 – 3rd and 10th
November 2016 – 1st, 11th, 15th, 16th, 21st to 25th, 29th and 30th
December 2016 – 16th to 31st

CA Resident Annual Pass:
Every Saturday and Sunday, plus:
May 2016 – 27th and 30th
June, July and August 2016 – All month
September 2016 – 2nd, 5th and 6th
October 2016 – 3rd and 10th
November 2016 – 11th and 21st to 25th
December 2016 – 16th to 31st
January 2017 – 10th
February 2017 – 20th
March 2017 – Saturdays and Sundays only

CA Resident Plus Annual Pass:
May 2016 – Every Saturday, plus the 1st, 22nd, 29th and 30th
June 2016 – 4th, 11th, 12th, 18th, 24th to 26th, 28th and 30th
July 2016 – All month
August 2016 – 1st to 15th, 20th, 21st, 27th and 28th
September 2016 – 3rd to 5th, 10th, 11th, 17th, 18th and 24th
October 2016 – 1st, 8th, 9th, 15th, 22nd, 23rd and 29th
November 2016 – 5th, 6th, and 24th to 26th
December 2016 – 4th, 10th, 17th to 31st
January 2017 – 1st, 15th and 16th
February 2017 – 12th, 18th and 19th

Gold Annual Pass
May 2016 – 1st, 28th and 29th
June 2016 – 18th, 25th and 26th
July 2016 –   Every Saturday and Sunday, plus the 4th
August 2016 – 6th, 7th, 13th, 14th and 20th
September 2016 – Every Saturday, plus the 4th
October 2016 – Every Saturday
November 2016 – 25th and 26th
December 2016 – 17th, 18th and 25th to 31st

There are no blackout dates for the Platinum Annual Pass.

Chapter 3

Accommodation

Many hotels are available near Universal Studios Hollywood and you are free to choose from the hundreds on offer in both the Hollywood area, downtown L.A. or further afield.

Below we have a selection of hotels. These are not operated by Universal itself, but are partner hotels. This means that you are able to book Universal package with tickets and the hotel together, which can save you money.

Room prices shown below are for a weekday off-peak date in November 2016. Prices during peak seasons are higher.

Hilton Universal City

Transportation: On-site. Free shuttle service. Can walk to Universal Studios.
Number of rooms: 495
Room prices: From $220 for a standard room.
Amenities: Convenience store, business center, café, fitness center, outdoor heated pool with hot tub, in-room dining, and Wi-Fi.

This 3.5-star hotel is ideally located just a 5-minute walk away from the theme park, or you can use the complimentary shuttle. The metro station is less than a 10-minute walk. Although pricey compared to some other options, you are paying for the excellent location and attention to service here. The outdoor pool, in particular, is great. Wi-Fi is an extra charge at this hotel. Parking is $28 per day ($40 for valet).

Dining:

Atrium Lounge – Snacks and drinks. Live piano music in the evening. Open 11:00am until late.

Café Sierra – Casual dining serving Chinese, Californian and continental cuisine. Also offers a seafood buffet on select days. Serves breakfast, lunch and dinner.

Coffee Corner – Coffee, sandwiches, paninis and gelato. Open for breakfast, lunch and dinner.

Sierra Pool Bar and Grill – Casual bites to eat by the pool such as burgers. Open 6:00am until 10:00pm.

Sheraton Universal Hotel

Transportation: On-site. Free shuttle service. Can walk to Universal Studios.

Number of rooms: 457

Room size: 325 ft² for a traditional guest room

Room prices: From $329 for a standard room

Amenities: Business center, fitness center, outdoor pool, in-room dining, and Wi-Fi.

Like the Hilton, the 3.5-star Sheraton is located on-site at Universal and is about 8-minutes' walk to the theme park, slightly further than the Hilton. Also known as the "Hotel of the Stars", customers are the number one priority at this hotel. As well as standard rooms, suites are also available to be booked at this hotel. Wi-Fi is an extra charge, but it is complimentary for loyalty club members. Parking is $28 per day ($32 for valet).

Dining:

In the Mix – Bar lounge serving drinks and light bites. Open midday until late.

Poolside Lounge – Poolside bar serving drinks and snacks. Open midday until mid-evening.
The California's – Indoor and outdoor American casual dining. Serves breakfast, lunch and dinner.

Loews Hollywood Hotel

Transportation: 1-stop away on the metro
Number of rooms: 628
Room size: 400 ft^2 for a standard room
Room prices: From $319 for a standard room
Amenities: Outdoor pool, full-service spa, fitness center, in-room dining and business center.

Located in Hollywood itself, and 1-minute from Hollywood Boulevard, the 4-star Loews Hollywood Hotel is the perfect location for seeing the stars. What's more, the hotel is just one stop on the metro from Universal Studios Hollywood – the total journey time from the hotel to the theme park is a mere 18 minutes. Complimentary Wi-Fi is available.

Dining:
Preston's – Contemporary American cuisine. Open for breakfast and lunch.
SPECK – Sandwiches and drinks. Open 11:00am to 5:00pm.
H2 Kitchen & Bar – Lounge bar. Open from early afternoon until late.

The Garland

Transportation: Trolley service to Universal Studios Hollywood
Number of rooms: 257
Room prices: From $215 for a standard room
Amenities: Wi-Fi, on-site restaurant and lounge, fitness center, outdoor pool, business center and valet parking.

This boutique hotel offers luxury just minutes from Universal Studios. Live the Hollywood lifestyle in this charming, retro-chic accommodation. A trolley service connects the hotel with Universal Studios Hollywood and the metro station in just five minutes; you can also walk to nearby restaurants and the theme park. Free Wi-Fi is available at this hotel. If we had to choose one hotel to stay at this would be it, even if it is slightly further away than the two on-property hotels.

Dining:
Front Yard – Table Service. Serves breakfast, lunch and dinner. As well brunch on weekends. Mains are $12-$16 at lunch and $13-$38 for dinner.
Front Yard to Go – In room dining or to take away. Includes breakfast, salads, burgers, steaks and more. Plus, large picnic style takeaway meals.
Lobby Bar – Poolside cocktails or lounge in the lobby.

Los Angeles Marriott Burbank Airport

Transportation: Complimentary scheduled shuttle service to Universal Studios. Must be reserved.
Number of rooms: 488
Room prices: Standard rooms from $229 per night
Amenities: On-site restaurant, outdoor pool, Wi-Fi, fitness center, valet parking and business center

Located right by Burbank airport, this 4-star hotel is convenient for anyone looking to stay a bit further out and be based by the airport. A complimentary scheduled shuttle service to Universal Studios Hollywood and the airport is available, though reservations are required. Wi-Fi is charged but Marriott Rewards members can get it for free.

Dining:
Daily Grill – Table Service. American-style. Open for breakfast, lunch and dinner.
Media Lounge – Sells Starbucks branded drinks and treats.

Sportsmen's Lodge Hotel

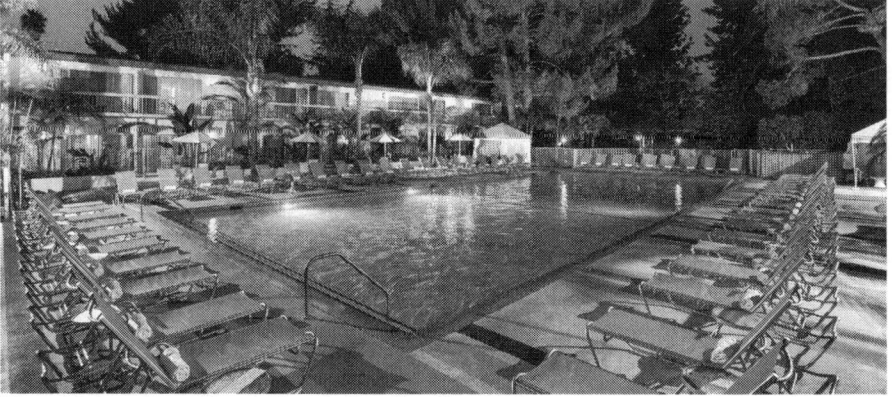

Transportation: Complimentary shuttle service
Number of rooms: 190
Room size: 300 ft² for a traditional guest room
Room prices: Standard rooms from $189 per night
Amenities: Wi-Fi, on-site restaurant and lounge, outdoor pool and business center.

A unique combination of rustic, San Fernando Valley charm and Tinseltown polish, the 3.5-star Sportsmen Lodge Hotel is just minutes away from the action of Universal Studios Hollywood by complimentary shuttle. This was once a haven for movie stars in the 50's, 60's and 70's. Wi-Fi is complimentary. There is no fitness suite at this hotel, but the pool is the largest in the San Fernando Valley.

Dining:
River Rock – Serves brunch and dinner, as well as a daily happy hour.
Patio Café – Breakfast and lunch options.
Pool Bar – Sip a cocktail by the huge pool.

Chapter 4

Getting There

Before we get too carried away with all the fun you can have at Universal Studios Hollywood, you must first make your way there. Here are some of your options:

By car

Universal Studios Hollywood is an easy 10-mile drive from downtown Los Angeles along the US-101 N. In low traffic conditions, this drive will take about 15 minutes, whereas during peak times it can take 45 minutes.

You should use "100 Universal City Plaza, Universal City, CA 91608" as the address for the parking garages.

There are five main parking areas at the resort. You should aim to park at the one that is closest to the main entrance. In order of proximity, they are: Frankenstein garage (closest), Woody Woodpecker outdoor lot (Preferred Parking and for disabled guests is located here), Jurassic Park garage, Curious George garage and finally the furthest is the ET garage.

With the exception of the Frankenstein lot, which is just by the park entrance, you will walk from all the other parking areas to the CityWalk entertainment area, and then to the theme park entrance itself.

Universal will begin redirecting traffic as these fill up. The furthest garage is about a 15 to 20-minute walk from your car to the park, whereas the closest is les than a 5-minute walk.

Parking is charged at Universal Studios Hollywood. General parking is $18, preferred parking is $25 and front gate parking is $40. Reduced prices operate for arrivals after 5:00pm. Valet parking is also available starting at $15 for staying under 2 hours.

Disneyland Resort to Universal Studios Hollywood by car:
Many visitors to Universal Studios Hollywood also spend time at the Disneyland Resort. The resorts are located on opposite sides of Los Angeles (35-miles apart) with a travel time of between 1 hour and 1 hour 30 minutes by car.

From Disneyland Resort you take the I-5 North, joining the US-101 North just outside downtown L.A. It is a simple drive.

Public Transportation

From Los Angeles International Airport (LAX):

LAX is not directly connected to the metro subway system. The easiest way to reach USH is therefore a combination of a bus and a subway ride. From LAX, you take the LAX FlyAway bus to Hollywood/Vine Station (buses depart hourly, journey time is about an hour). From Hollywood/Vine, you take the subway (Metro Red Line) to Universal City Station, where you can get a shuttle bus to Universal Studios Hollywood. The total journey time is about 1 hour 30 minutes, costing $9.75 per person.

From Downtown Los Angeles:

Universal Studios Hollywood is well connected with public transport. Universal City station is located on the subway Metro Red Line. Travel time from Union Station in downtown LA to Universal City station is about 25 minutes. You can get a TAP card to use on the Metro from a vending machine in the station for $1 and then load it with credit. A one-way trip on the metro is priced at $1.75.

Once at Universal City station, there is a free Universal Studios shuttle that runs every 10 to 15 minutes. Shuttle service begins at 7:00am every morning. Service continues until approximately 2 hours after the theme park closes.

From Disneyland Resort:

As the Disneyland Resort is located in Orange County, it is not served by a Metro service, which makes travelling from the Disneyland Resort to Universal Studios Hollywood longer than necessary. It is, however, doable.

First of all, you will need to take a bus from the Disneyland Main Transportation Center to ARTIC (a transport hub including bus station and Anaheim Station for trains). Bus routes 14, 15 and 22 serve this station. This will take about 10 minutes.

Once at ARTIC/Anaheim Station, you can either take the Pacific Surfliner Amtrak train (a long-distance service) or the Metrolink Orange County Line (a regional service) into L.A. Union Station. This part of the journey will take about 45 minutes.

At Union Station in downtown L.A., you get the Metro Red Line to 'Universal/Studio City Station' and then get the shuttle bus up to the theme park, as mentioned in the previous section. You can count on a journey of 25 minutes on the metro, plus 5 to 20 minutes on the shuttle, depending on how long you wait.

The total journey time for the trip, including waiting for trains is usually 2 hours 30 minutes to 3 hours 30 minutes. We recommend using www.metro.net to plan your journey and get exact timings.

Be sure to check the schedule for the train part of your trip (Orange County Line or Pacific Surfliner), to avoid being stranded in L.A. on the way back to Disneyland as services end early in the day. At the time of writing, the last train on weekdays leaves L.A. Union Station at 6:35pm, and on weekends it is at 4:40pm. These trains are also infrequent, compared to the buses and the metro.

The total cost of this time by public transportation is about $25. You will need exact change for the bus portion of this journey.

If there are several of you travelling together, we would recommend making this journey by taxi, as it will be quicker, simpler and cheaper.

Shuttle Services
From LAX:
We do not know of any commercial shuttles between LAX and Universal Studios Hollywood. A chartered car quote from Supershuttle.com comes in at around $80-$120 for the car, plus tip.

From Downtown LA:
We do not know of any commercial shuttles between LAX and Universal Studios Hollywood. We would recommend taking the Metro Red Line subway service, which takes 25 minutes to Universal from Downtown LA. See the public transportation section for more details.

Disneyland Resort to Universal Studios Hollywood by shuttle:
There is one daily shuttle service that runs from the Anaheim area hotels to Universal Studios Hollywood. You can either purchase transportation on its own, or a transportation option with Universal park tickets included. The transportation only option is $30 for a round-trip ticket. The price including entry into the park is $121 per adult. This service is run by **www.LuxBusAmerica.com**.

Taxis
From LAX:
A taxi from LAX to Universal Studios Hollywood will cost you between $60 and $90 on average for the 26-mile journey, depending on traffic conditions.

We highly recommend using ride-sharing company Uber. With Uber, the fare estimate is $34 to $45 for this journey. Visit http://uber.com/invite/uberindependentguides or use the promotion code "uberindependentguides" to get a $15 free credit for your first journey. You will need to download the Uber app onto your smartphone and create an account.

From Downtown LA:
A taxi from near Union Station to Universal Studios Hollywood will cost between $30 and $40. The estimated Uber fare for this journey is $12 to $17. If you use our promotional code above, chances are this will cover all (or most) of this journey. This is a 9-mile journey, lasting about 15 minutes when there is no traffic. Fares will be higher with traffic.

Disneyland Resort to Universal Studios Hollywood by taxi:
Finally, Disneyland to Universal Studios by taxi is a lengthy 36-mile journey, which usually takes 1 hour to 1 hour 30 minutes depending on traffic. A taxi fare for this journey is usually about $110 to $130. The equivalent estimated Uber fare is $40 to $54.

Chapter 5

Universal Studios Hollywood - Park Guide

Universal Studios Hollywood is a relatively small theme park with fewer than twenty attractions in total. Due to space constraints, however, the attraction selection has to be very strong – and it is. There are no poor attractions that standout, and those present are all fantastic. As the park is small, you should be able to comfortably complete it in one day.

Note: Average attraction waits noted in this section are estimates for busy summer days and on school break. Wait times may be lower at other times of the year. They may also occasionally be higher, especially during the week of 4th July, Thanksgiving, Christmas, New Year and other public holidays.

Where we list food prices, this information was accurate during our last visit to the restaurant. We also do not post the full menu but just a sample of the food on offer. Meal prices listed do not include a drink, unless otherwise stated. When an attraction is listed as requiring lockers, all loose items must be stored in complimentary lockers outside each attraction.

Park Entrance area

The park entrance area is the gateway to Universal Studios Hollywood. You pass through it to get to the rest of the park, and you walk through it again when exiting.

This area is where **Guest Relations** is located where you can get help with disability passes, questions, positive feedback and complaints. Guest Relations is located to the right-hand side after the turnstiles. This area also has locker rentals, as well as stroller and wheelchair rentals.

First Aid is located along the Upper Lot area next to the theater housing Animal Actors. Another First Aid station is located next to Jurassic Park: The Ride.

Upper Lot

The Upper Lot is the main part of the park, with the park entrance and contains the most attractions. This area is also directly connected to the brand new Wizarding World of Harry Potter. At the end of the Upper Lot, you will find escalators and elevators (dubbed 'The StarWay') taking you down to the Lower Lot and the attractions located there.

Despicable Me: Minion Mayhem

Height Restriction: Guests under 40 inches (1.02m) may not ride. Those between 40 inches and 48 inches (1.22m) must ride accompanied. Guests over 48 inches may ride alone.

Attraction length: 4 minutes + 2 pre-shows totaling 12 minutes

Front of the Line Access: Yes

Average Wait: 30 to 60 minutes

Lockers required: No

Despicable Me' fans can take part in Minion training in this simulator ride experience. The queue line pre-show rooms are very well done. Queues are shorter for this ride in the morning, as it is somewhat hidden.

Top Tip: For those who do not like simulator movement, a stationary version of this attraction is offered where you sit in benches at the front of the theater room. These do not move, but you still get to watch the same 3D movie.

Super Silly Fun Land

Height Restriction: 48 inches (1.22m) maximum
Average Wait: None. Walkthrough area.
Front of the Line Access: No
Lockers required: No

Based on a seaside funfair from the Despicable Me films, this play area is split into two parts – a standard playground with no water, and a water-filled play area. There are changing rooms available for visitors to get changed into swimwear if they wish. This is an open area of the park, with no queue lines.

Silly Swirly

Height Restriction: 48 inches (1.22m) minimum to ride alone. Riders under 48 inches must be accompanied by someone aged 14 or older.
Attraction length: 1 minute 30 seconds
Front of the Line Access: No
Lockers required: No
Average Wait: 10 to 25 minutes

This is a fairly standard fairground style ride that is part of Super Silly Fun Land. It is similar to the Dumbo rides at Disney parks. Here you sit in a bug and go around in a circle; you can control the height of your bug using a joystick inside the vehicle. As it is so hidden away, waits for most of the year stay under 10 minutes, possibly peaking at 25 minutes on very busy days.

Shrek 4D

Height Restriction: None. No handheld infants.
Attraction length: 12 minutes for the main show + 5 minutes for pre-show
Front of the Line Access: Yes
Average Wait: 15 to 45 minutes
Lockers required: No

Stepping into Shrek 4D, you know you are getting into a different kind of attraction – it is not just a 3D, but a 4D experience. The unique part of this attraction is the seats, which act like personal simulators. For those not wishing to experience the seat movement, a limited number of stationary seats are also available on the back two rows – these are clearly marked. The film itself is great fun with some corny jokes and jabs at Disney thrown in for good measure.

Animal Actors: On Location

Show length: 20 minutes
Front of the Line Access: Yes
Lockers required: No

A behind the scenes look at how animals are taught to act in films, including audience participation. It is not our favourite show in the park, but animal fans will enjoy this. You will not need to generally turn up more than fifteen minutes in advance to secure a spot as this is not a hugely popular show.

Special Effects Show
Show length: 20 to 25 minutes
Front of the Line Access: Yes
Lockers required: No
This is one of our favourite shows at the park, featuring a fun and educational insight into how special effects and stunts are used in the making of movies. The show is funny and if you are in the queue line early enough you may even be cast to participate, if you wish. You will generally not need to arrive at the theater any earlier than fifteen minutes before the show begins, as there are a huge number of seats.

WaterWorld

Show length: 20 minutes
Front of the Line Access: Yes
Lockers required: No
Despite being based on one of Hollywood's biggest flops, WaterWorld is constantly rated as the best show in the park by visitors. This stunt show features a whole load of pyrotechnics, fire, water effects and many surprises throughout. Actions fans are sure to be in for a treat! Beware of the wet zone, where you will get splashed a fair few times. The auditorium for this show is the largest in the park, but it is also a very popular choice; be in the queue at least 15 minutes before show time to get a seat.

Universal Studio Tour

Height Restriction: None. There are some very intense moments, however.
Attraction length: 45 to 60 minutes
Front of the Line Access: Yes
Average Wait: 40 to 75 minutes
Lockers required: No

The park's star attraction, the Universal Studio Tour is the reason why the park was founded. Well before USH was a theme park, the Studio Tour operated as a single attraction, allowing guests to visit parts of Universal's studios. Now, it is one of several attractions in the park, but still remains hugely popular and is one of the main reasons why many guests pay the theme park a visit.

The ride takes place in huge trams, with rows seating six people, which take you on a non-stop tour lasting between 45 and 60 minutes. The exact length of this experience depends on access conditions and whether all segments of the tour are operational. A live guide narrates the experience and Jimmy Fallon appears on screen in the trams once in a while to add more detail.

On some sections of the tour you going past soundstages and other sets used for production, whereas other parts of the tour have mini attractions that have been created exclusively for the tram tour, such as the immersive 360-degree experience starring King Kong.

Every few years, a section of the tour changes. Current sets include: Colonial Street (Wisteria Lane), The Front Lot, Little Europe, Metropolitan New York Sets, The Old West (Six Points Texas), War of the Worlds and Whoville.

As well as the sets, there are following staged events throughout the tour: Jurassic Park, Old Mexico: Flash Flood, JAWS, Earthquake: The Big One, Psycho: Bates Motel, KONG 360 and Fast & Furious: Supercharged.

We will not go into any more detail as to what happens in each of these segments so as to maintain an air of surprise. Some sections of the tour are intense, and there is a chance you may get wet.

You should expect wait times for this attraction to build up very quickly, from park opening, peaking in early afternoon.

As the tour is such a complex logistical operation, it closes earlier than the rest of the park. The last tour generally departs 1 hour 40 minutes before park closing, though the exact timing will be displayed at the attraction entrance and wait time signs throughout the park.

Tours are in English, though there are also tours in Spanish and Mandarin available at select times. Check your times guide for the timing of these.

On select dates, the Nighttime Studio Tour is also offered with the same content as the day tour, except for some very minor changes.

A VIP Tour option is also available. More details later in this guide.

The Simpsons Ride

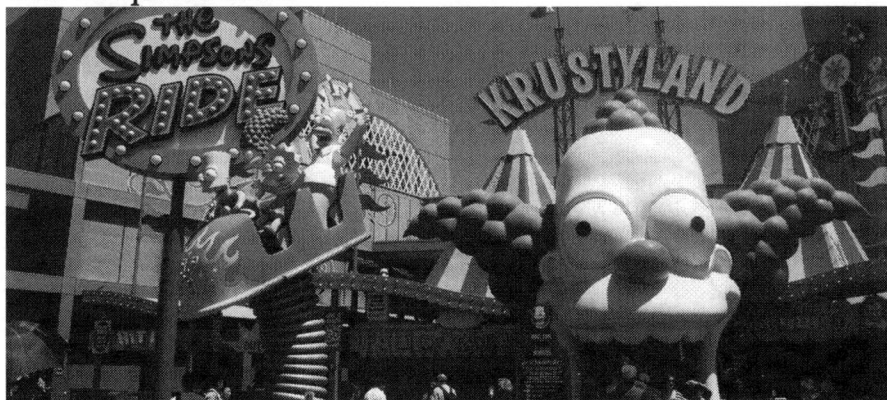

Height Restriction: Guests under 40 inches (1.02m) may not ride. Those between 40 inches and 48 inches (1.22m) must ride accompanied. Guests over 48 inches may ride alone.
Attraction length: 5 minutes + two pre-shows = 20 minutes total
Front of the Line Access: Yes

Average Wait: 45 to 80 minutes
Lockers required: No
The Simpsons Ride is a fun-filled rollercoaster simulator where you try and escape the maniacal Sideshow Bob. Your adventure is filled with gags throughout and is a fun family experience. Simpsons fans will love it!

Springfield U.S.A. Restaurants:
- **Moe's Tavern** sells Flaming Moes and Duff Beer. Be sure to check out The Love Tester Machine.
- **Luigi's Pizza** sells personal-sized pizzas.
- **Cletus' Chicken Shack** sells fried chicken and chicken sandwiches.
- **Krusty Burger** sells burgers, hot dogs and Buzz Cola.
- **Bumblebee Man's Taco Truck** sells tacos, nachos and beer.
- **Duff Brewery Beer Garden** sells refreshing Duff beer.
- **Lard Lad's Donuts** sells donuts and coffee.
- **Phineas Q. Butterfat's Ice Cream** sells ice creams and sundaes.
- **Sud McDuff's Hot Dogs** sells hot dogs, pretzels, churros and more.

Upper Lot Restaurants:
Cinnabon – Serves cinnamon rolls, ice cream, coffee and other drinks.
Despicable Delights – Serves Freeze Ray Smoothies, cotton candy and more.
French Street Bistro – Serves sandwiches, salads, pastries and Starbucks drinks.
Gru's Lab Café – Serves nachos, rotisserie chicken, sandwiches and salads.
Mulligan's Pub & Spirits – A pub serving alcoholic and non-alcoholic drinks.
Palace Theatre Café – Serves sandwiches, salads, turkey legs, rotisserie chicken, burritos and soups. Operates seasonally.
Plaza Grill – Serves breakfast until 11:00. After this, you can find burgers, sandwiches, turkey legs, salads, fries, root beer floats and funnel cakes.

The Wizarding World of Harry Potter

Step into the world of Harry Potter and experience what it is like to visit Hogsmeade. Dine, visit the shops and experience the wild rides. The area is incredibly well themed and Potter fans will see authenticity unlike anywhere else. Throughout this section, you may see The Wizarding World of Harry Potter abbreviated to WWOHP.

The WWOHP is the brand new area in Universal Studios Hollywood, having opened its doors on April 7th, 2016. It follows the successful launch of Wizarding Worlds at Universal's parks in Florida and Japan.

Fun Fact: The attention to detail here is stunning. For example, in the restrooms at the Wizarding World, you can hear Moaning Myrtle.

Triwizard Tournament

A six-minute dance contest between two competing wizard schools: men versus women. The men's routine involves complex sword-fighting techniques, while the ladies dazzle with their ribbons and acrobatics. It is a nice bit of entertainment, and a great photo opportunity.

Frog Choir

A thirteen-minute series of songs inspired by the the Harry Potter movies performed by Hogwarts students and their frogs, all done a capella with voices and no instruments. There is an almost beat-box flair to this show and it is a great piece of live entertainment.

Flight of the Hippogriff

Height Restriction: Guests under 39 inches (0.99m) may not ride. Those between 39 inches and 48 inches (1.22m) may ride with a companion.

Attraction length: 1 minute 20 seconds
Front of the Line Access: Yes
Average Wait: 60 to 90 minutes
Lockers required: No
A small rollercoaster where you soar on a Hippogriff and go past Hagrid's hut and motorcycle, as well as Buckbeak. Good family fun and a good starter coaster before putting your children on the likes of *Revenge of the Mummy*. The ride reaches speeds of 40mph, so it does get reasonably fast.

Harry Potter and the Forbidden Journey

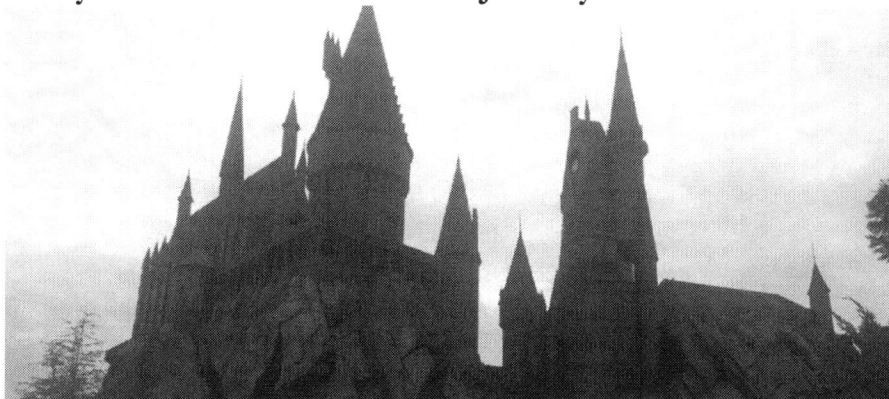

Height Restriction: 48 inches (1.22m)
Attraction length: 5 minutes
Front of the Line Access: Yes
Average Wait: 60 to 120 minutes
Lockers required: Yes
Harry Potter fans will freak out over this enchanting ride. From the breathtaking moment your enchanted bench starts flying your experience with Harry begins. Along the way you will take part in a Quidditch tournament, encounter a dragon, see the Womping Willow, be approached by Dementors and much more. The ride combines physicals sets with 3D screens for an incredibly immersive experience. The queue line is almost an attraction in itself.

If you do not wish to experience the ride, you can still explore the inside of Hogwarts castle, simply ask one of the team members for the Tour Only entrance. This allows you to skip the locker queue line and bring cameras to take photos of the incredibly well-themed interior.

A Single Rider queue line is available, though it skips most of the detailed interiors. This can cut down wait times significantly; waits in this queue are usually about 50-75% shorter than the standard wait time in our experience, though this varies.

This is the star attraction at the Wizarding World and we expect it to keep long wait times for the next few years.

Warning: We have found that this ride creates an incredible amount of mental strain due to the simulated sensations and the realism of the screens in front of you. The 3D glasses only add to this. This means that if you ride it more than once back-to-back, you are likely to feel unwell.

Hidden Secret: When you are in Dumbledore's office hearing his speech, take a look at the books on the wall to the right of him. Once in a while, one of the books may just do something very magical.

Hidden Secret 2: Look at the moving portraits of the four founders of Hogwarts; each of them is holding a Horcrux used to defeat Voldemort in the films and books.

Ollivanders:

Height Restriction: None
Attraction length: 3 to 4 minutes
Front of the Line Access: No
Average Wait: 30 to 60 minutes
Technically, this is a pre-show to a shop. You enter Ollivanders in groups of about 25 people. One person in the group will be chosen by the wandmaster to find the right wand for them. Eventually the right one is found and they are given the opportunity to buy it when the group is moved to the shop area next door. This is a fantastic experience that we highly recommend you visit. It is suitable for people of all ages.

Interactive Wand Experiences:

An interactive wand experience is available at the Wizarding World. In order to participate, guests must purchase an interactive wand from the Wizarding World's shops. These are priced at $48; $8 more than the non-interactive wands.

Once you have purchased a wand, look for the bronze medallions embedded in the streets that mark the various locations where you can cast spells. A map of the locations is included with each wand.

Once you are standing on a medallion, perform the correct spell. Simply draw the shape of the spell in the air with your wand and saying the name of the spell. Then, watch the magic come to life.

This is a really fun bit of extra entertainment, especially as the wands can be reused again and again during future visits.

Character Meets and Drinks:

To maintain the integrity of the Harry Potter areas, J.K. Rowling, the author of the Harry Potter books, specified that no branded drinks be sold in the Wizarding World – so, you will not find Coca Cola products here, for example. You will only find Harry Potter branded drinks such as Butterbeer, water and some fruit squashes. You are, of course, free to buy a drink elsewhere in the park, and bring it into the Wizarding World.

J.K. Rowling also prohibited character meets. So, you cannot meet Harry, Hermione, Hagrid, Draco, Ron or other characters from the films in the Wizarding World.

Restaurants:

The restaurants in Hogsmeade are incredibly well-themed and the Quick Service food here is among the best in the park. We highly recommend you take a look inside the Hog's Head and Three Broomsticks, even if you do not plan on eating there.

- **Hog's Head Pub** – This pub is located in the same building as the Three Broomsticks. Serves alcoholic beer, a selection of spirits, non-alcoholic Butterbeer and juices.
- **Three Broomsticks** – Serves breakfast meals. At lunch and dinner, you will find Cornish pasties, fish & chips, Shepherd's pie, smoked turkey legs, rotisserie smoked chicken and spareribs. Plus, desserts including Butterbeer potted cream.
- **The Magic Neep and Ice Cream Cart** – This small cart sells bottled drinks, beers, pre-packaged ice cream and fresh fruit.

Shops:

The shops and merchandise in the Wizarding World are just as much of an experience as some of the rides. Be sure to step inside to admire the detail, and maybe even purchase a souvenir or two. Shops in the area include:

- **Filch's Emporium of Confiscated Goods** – Inside you will find themed apparel, mugs, photo frames and trinkets. It has almost everything a Harry Potter fan could ever want, and even sells Marauder's Maps.
- **Honeydukes** – For those with a sweet tooth, make sure to visit Honeydukes. You will find love Bertie Bott's Every-Flavour Beans, chocolate frogs (with collectable trading cards), and tons of other candy.
- **Dervish & Banges** – The place to come for Hogwarts uniforms, as well as stationary and Quidditch items.
- **The Owl Post** – A real post office where your letters or postcards can be sent to friends and family; these will get a Hogsmeade postmark and a Harry Potter stamp. You will also find stationary on sale here, as well as owl toys.
- **Gladrag's Wizard Wear** – Sells wizard apparel, including hats and accessories, as well as jewelry.
- **Hogwarts Express Photo Opportunity** – Get a photo taken inside a carriage from the Hogwarts Express. The first photo is $24.95, with additional photos costing $5 each.
- **Ollivander's Wand Shop** – Purchase a unique Ollivander's wand, or choose from character replica wands.
- **Wizeacre's Wizarding Equipment** – Find all kinds of wizardry essentials here. From hourglasses to compasses, and telescopes to binoculars. Plus, themed apparel.
- **Zonko's Joke Shop** – This shop features all kinds of prank-filled items and toys, as well as novelty items and magic tricks, including Extendable Ears, Decoy Detonators and Fangled Flyers.

Note: The official Harry Potter branded wands are pricey; expect to pay $40 a piece for regular wands and $48 for interactive ones.

Crowd Control Measures and The Return Ticket system:

J. K. Rowling specifically requested that the buildings in the *Wizarding World* be made the scale. As such, this area of the park is relatively small and can only accommodate a few thousand people (we have hard it has a capacity of 6,000 people at a time).

During periods of peak attendance at the park, Universal may implement a return ticket system as a crowd control measure. It is not possible to know in advance if either of these systems will be used – if you are visiting around a major holiday, though, there is a high chance.

With the return ticket system, you go to a kiosk on Universal Plaza, select a return time and get a free return ticket to come back and enter the *Wizarding World*. Only one person needs to go to the kiosk and they will simply need to touch the screen and choose a return time. No park tickets are required to do this. Universal Team Members will be available to direct you.

On days when this crowd control measure is in place, expect very high wait times for all attractions within the land – this means 90 to 120 minutes for the *Forbidden Journey*, and 60 minutes for everything else. The crowd control measure is merely a way of limiting the number of people in the land.

The system will only be in operation when the lands have reached full capacity. So, you may find that during certain hours you need a return ticket to get in, but not during others.

Lower Lot

Once you have made it down the escalator (dubbed 'StarWay') to the Lower Lot you will find a few attractions, including some of the park's best.

Along the StarWay there are several viewing areas, so be make sure to take in the views across the San Fernando Valley. You will be able to see other studios nearby including Warner Bros and Walt Disney Animation. Make sure to get some photos and use the plaques nearby to learn about what you can see from this unique viewpoint.

TRANSFORMERS: The Ride-3D

Height Restriction: 40 inches (1.02m). Riders between 40 inches and 48 inches (1.22m) must ride accompanied by a supervising companion.
Attraction length: 4 minutes 30 seconds
Front of the Line Access: Yes
Average Wait: 60 to 120 minutes
Lockers required: No
TRANSFORMERS is a 3D screen-based moving ride, similar to *The Amazing Adventures of Spiderman* in *Universal's Islands of Adventure*. The combination of real sets with well-blended, immersive screens makes for an experience unlike any other. The storyline follows the Autobots trying to get the Allspark and, of course, you get caught in the midst of the action. The ride is an enjoyable experience and action fans will love the non-stop nature of this ride. This ride often has one of the longest queues in the park outside of the Wizarding World. A Single Rider line is available.

Revenge of the Mummy

Height Restriction: 48 inches (1.22m)
Attraction length: 2 minutes
Front of the Line Access: Yes
Average Wait: 20 to 60 minutes
Lockers required: Yes

An incredibly unique rollercoaster featuring fire, smoke, forward motion, backwards motion, and much more. The whole ride is fantastic and is one of the most fun coasters we have been on, starting off as a dark ride and developing into a coaster.

Although the ride does not go upside down, and is not exactly the fastest attraction in California (though it does hit 45mph in less than two seconds), it does tell its story very well and really immerses you in the atmosphere. It is a great thrill, with plot twists throughout.

The queue line is also detailed and sets the tone before even arriving at the ride station. This is one the park's two rollercoasters (the other being *Flight of the Hippogriff*) and it can get significant waits throughout the day.

If you have ridden the attraction with the same name at Universal Studios Florida, unfortunately this is a pared down version that is just not as good. This was due to the limited space available for construction. It is still, however, very enjoyable and it is interesting to compared the similarities and differences.

A Single Rider line is available.

Jurassic Park: The Ride

Height Restriction: 42 inches (1.07m). Riders between 42 inches and 48 inches (1.22m) must ride accompanied by a supervising companion.
Attraction length: 7 minutes
Front of the Line Access: Yes
Average Wait: 30 to 60 minutes
Lockers required: Optional
Step into the world of Jurassic Park on a river boat, glide past huge dinosaurs, and enter through enormous doors just like in the movies. However, this calm river adventure soon changes course. Watch out for the T-Rex before you come splashing down an 84-foot drop! A Single Rider line is available.
Top Tip: You won't stay dry on this ride, but the driest seats are at the back.

Note: Lockers are not compulsory for this ride, so be prepared to pay for lockers if you want to make keep your stuff dry. During the winter months (January to March), the ride is often unavailable for scheduled maintenance.

Dino Play
Height Restriction: 48 inches (1.20m) maximum
Front of the Line Access: No
This play area themed to Jurassic Park contains dinosaur fossils and footprints for those not old enough to visit the mammoth water attraction next door. There are no water elements to the play area.

Lower Lot Restaurants:
Ben and Jerry's Ice Cream – Serves ice cream.
Jurassic Café – Serves personal pizzas, burgers, roasted chicken, and salads.
Panda Express – Asian inspired food, including orange chicken and sushi.
Starbucks Coffee – Serves Starbucks drinks, pastries and snacks.

Universal Studios Hollywood Park Entertainment

In addition to the live shows, such as WaterWorld listed in the attraction section, there are also a variety of character meet and greets on offer throughout Universal Studios Hollywood.

You will find characters in areas appropriate to them, for example, to meet Optimus Prime, head to near Transformers: The Ride. Many characters also meet in the Universal Plaza area. Characters that you will often find throughout the park include:

- Optimus Prime, Bumbleebee and Megatron (from Transformers)
- The Minions, Gru & Margo (from Despicable Me)
- The Simpsons
- SpongeBob SquarePants – Near Universal Plaza
- Shrek, Princess Fiona and Donkey
- Curious George – Near Cartooniversal
- Raptor Encounter – Includes a short show as the dinosaur is brought out and when it returns to its paddock at the end of meeting guests.
- Scooby-Doo and Shaggy – Universal Plaza
- Curious George – Near Cartooniversal
- Marilyn Monroe – By Universal Studio Tour
- Woody and Winnie Woodpecker – Near Cartooniversal

Other characters you may see include: Dora the Explorer, Dracula, Doc Brown, Beetlejuice, Frankenstein, and more.

Character times are printed on your park map and are also available live via the USH website at **www.ushwaittimes.com**. Other characters will also appear throughout the park without specific public schedules.

Unlike character meet and greets at the nearby Disneyland Resort, character appearances at Universal Studios Hollywood do not usually require any form of forward planning or queueing. There may be a few people ahead of you to meet the characters but we have never waited more than five minutes.

There are no parades at Universal Studios Hollywood.

Chapter 7

Universal CityWalk

Universal's CityWalk is located just outside the theme parks, and within walking distance of all the nearby hotels. There are stores, restaurants, a movie theater and other forms of entertainment.

CityWalk is free to all visitors and no admission ticket is required. Parking is at the main Universal parking garages. CityWalk has ATMs, wheelchair rentals ($7 with valid ID), lockers and a lost and found facility.

To get the latest CityWalk opening hours, and details on any live entertainment that may be taking place during your visit, check out **www.citywalkhollywood.com**. You can also call 818-622-4455 for additional information.

Dining
CityWalk is filled with unique dining experiences, as well as well-known chains. This section helps you choose where to eat on your next visit.

There are numerous Quick Service dining options:
Ben & Jerry's Ice Cream, Cinnabon, The Coffee Bean & Tea Leaf, The Crepe Café, The Flame Broiler, Jamba Juice, KFC Express/Pizza Hut Express, Panda Express, Pink's Famous Hot Dogs, Popcornopolis, Smashburger, Starbucks Coffee, Subway, Taco Bell, Wetzel's Pretzels and Yogurtland.

There are also many Table Service dining options at CityWalk:

Bubba Gump Shrimp Company, Buca di Beppo, Camacho's Cantina, Hard Rock Café, Johnny Rockets Burgers & Shakes, Karl Strauss Brewing Company, Saddle Ranch Chop House, Samba Brazilian Steakhouse & Lounge, Tony Roma's, Wasabi and Wolfgang Puck Bistro.

Reservations for Table Service establishments can be made at opentable.com or by calling restaurants directly.

Top Tip: From Monday to Friday from 11:00 to 15:00, visitors can enjoy the "Shop, Dine and Play" promotion which reduces parking to $2 for the first two hours, $15 from 2-4 hours and $30 for stays of over 4 hours. Parking can be validated at any participating CityWalk restaurant, retail or entertainment venue excluding AMC CityWalk Cinemas.

Movie Theater

CityWalk features an AMC Universal Cineplex with 19 screens, including one that shows films in 7-story IMAX.

Tickets prices vary depending on the time of day and several other factors. A general ticket for an adult is priced at $7.25 to $14.25. Child tickets are for kids ages 2 to 12. Senior tickets (over 60) and student ticket (13+ with a valid ID) discounts are also available.

Top Tip: If you watch a movie at the AMC movie theater at CityWalk, you get a rebate on your parking, reducing it to just $5. The rebate is done at the AMC box office.

iFly Indoor Skydiving

If you fancy an extra thrill, why not go for an indoor skydive? No experience is necessary and the experience is available for ages 3 and up. Pricing starts at $60 for two short flights, with many price points going up to $600 for twenty-four flights. Pictures and videos of your experience are available for an extra charge, though some packages include video footage.

If you're not flying, take a walk by anyway as the wind-chamber has a glass side so you can see all the action from the main walking paths at CityWalk.

Shopping

If you fancy some shopping, there are plenty of places to visit including:

Abercrombie & Fitch, ANGL, Billabong, Bubba Gump Shrimp Store, Crow's Nest Toys, The Dodgers Clubhouse, Element, Flip Flop Shops, Fossil, Francesca's Collection, GUESS Accessories, Hard Rock Store, Hot Topic, IT'SUGAR, Lids, Locker Room (by Lids), The Los Angeles Sock Market, LUSH Cosmetics, Magnet Max, The Raider Image, SCENE, Sketchers, Sparky's, Things From Another World, Universal Studio Store and Upstart Crow.

Universal CityWalk Nightlife:

After a dinner, some shopping or a skydive, you may want to opt to party the night away at one of three bars or nightclubs.

Howl at the Moon features live music, a dance party and huge drinks.

Saddle Ranch Chop House is a high energy rock-western experience, serving food and drinks. This not-to-be missed location has three bars, inside and outside seating and even has two mechanical bulls. Open daily, with dance nights held Thursday through Saturday from 10:30pm.

Samba Brazilian Steakhouse and Lounge provides delicious south-American fare and relaxed vibes in the lounge area. Enjoy happy hour from 4:00pm to 7:00pm daily, and live dancers every hour from 7:00pm to 9:00pm.

The 5 Towers plaza is an outdoor concert venue in the center of CityWalk that regularly features live bands and other acts.

Out of state visitors in particular should be aware that the minimum drinking age in California is 21 and anyone aged under 30 will be ID-ed.

Somewhat surprisingly for many visitors, there is even a law-imposed curfew for under-18s. Under Los Angeles law it is unlawful "for any minor under the age of eighteen (18) years to be present in or upon any... public ground, public place or public building, place of amusement or eating place, vacant lot, or unsupervised place between the hours of 10:00 p.m. on any day and sunrise of the immediately following day". This is waived if they are accompanied by an adult. CityWalk security are very much present in the evenings and this law is strictly enforced.

Chapter 8

Services

In-Park and Ride Photos

Characters located around the park are often accompanied by an in-park photographer; sometimes these members of staff will also be present throughout the park by major landmarks too. The photographers will happily use your cameras to take photos and will also take an "official" photo with their own camera. You will be given a slip of paper with your photo number on. At any time until the end of the day, you can view all your in-park photos at the Photo Center in the entrance area of the park.

On-ride photos function differently and can be purchased by the ride exit after having ridden the attraction. Rides that include on-ride photos are: The Simpsons Ride, Revenge of the Mummy, and Jurassic Park: The Ride.

Ride Lockers

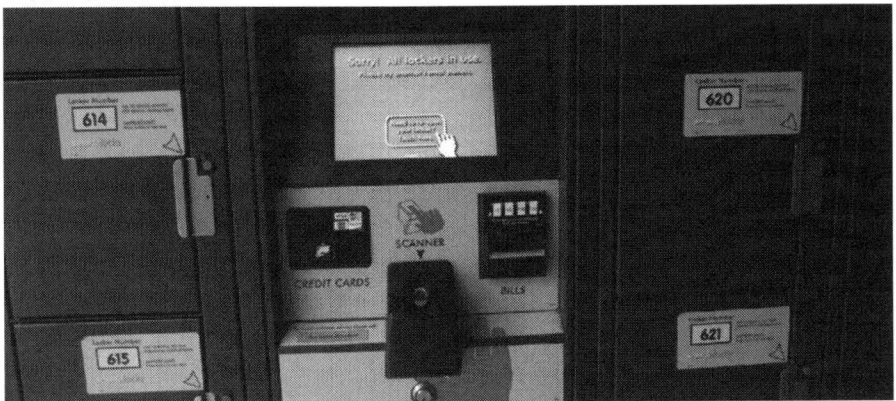

Two of the rides at USH – *Harry Potter and the Forbidden Journey* and *Revenge of the Mummy* – do not allow you to take your belongings onto them; loose articles must be placed in free lockers. Here is how they work:

- Approach a locker station located by the entrance to these rides;
- Select 'Rent a locker' from the touch screen;
- Put your fingerprint on the reader and you will be assigned a locker to put your stuff in;
- Go to the locker, put your belongings inside and press the green button next to the locker to lock the door. It is very important that you do this to make sure the locker is actually locked! If you forget to press the green button, the locker will automatically lock 5 seconds after the door is closed.

The lockers are free for a certain period of time. This is always longer than the current posted attraction wait time. For example, a 90-minute queue for *Forbidden Journey* would typically allow you 120 or 150 minutes of locker rental time to allow you to queue, experience the ride and collect your belongings without having to worry.

If you keep your stuff in the lockers longer than the free period, charges apply.

As well as the free lockers, larger paid-for ride lockers are also available to rent here. For the majority of people, though, these won't be necessary.

Lockers for *Jurassic Park: The Ride* are optional and not free.

Top Tip 1: If you rent a locker and your free time has expired because the line took longer than expected, tell a Team Member who will sort out the issue.

Top Tip 2: If you forget your locker number, there is a feature on the locker terminals that will help you find it.

Top Tip 3: Lockers for water rides are not free. In this case you could simply walk to a locker for another ride where they are free. This can save you a decent amount of money over the course of a trip. *Revenge of the Mummy* is close enough to *Jurassic Park: The Ride* and often has long locker rental times, for example.

Top Tip 4: The touchscreens on the lockers are unresponsive, meaning that it can be hard for the touchscreen to register your finger touches. We recommend using your fingernails to touch the screen to solve this problem.

All-day park locker rentals:
Non-ride specific lockers are located by the entry plaza – the cost varies depending on the size of locker required:
Locker sizes are as follows:
- $8 Lockers: Height – 12¾", Width – 11" and Length – 16½"
- $12 Lockers: Height – 16", Width – 8" and Length – 16"
- $15 Lockers: Height – 21½", Width – 11" and Length – 16"
- $20 Lockers: Height – 18", Width – 18" and Length – 36"

The lockers accept both cash and credit/debit cards. Guests may access these lockers as many times as they want throughout the day.

Front of the Line Pass

If you are willing to pay to get on rides quicker, then Universal's Front of the Line Pass (also known as a Gate A pass) is perfect for you.

The Front of the Line (FOTL) Pass allows you to skip the regular queue lines at almost every attraction. You will be able to enter a separate queue line that is significantly shorter than the regular queue and drastically reduce your wait times. For shows, you will be allowed entry before guests who do not have an FOTL Pass – usually 15 minutes before the show is due to begin. There will be a reserved seating area. You may only use your faster access privileges once per participating attraction.

The FOTL pass cannot be purchased as a standalone item; it is bundled with a park ticket for one all-inclusive price.

What does it cost?
Pricing varies according to how busy the theme park is. Tickets can be bought in advance online or at the theme park entrance. Remember the price of your FOTL pass includes admission, as well as your faster access privileges. The more expensive the FOTL ticket, the more useful it will be.

	Low Season	**Mid Season**	**High Season**	**Peak Season**
Adult	$179	$199 to $209	$219 to $229	$239

Which rides are not included?
FOTL Passes are valid on all attractions at the theme parks, with the following exceptions: *Ollivanders* and *Silly Swirl*. *Triwizard Tournament* and the *Frog Choir* shows do not require advanced access and you can simply walk into. In addition, play areas such as *Dino Play* and *Super Silly Fun Land* do not have faster access as there are no queue lines to enter these.

How do I use it?
When at an attraction, look for the Gate A entrance. This will usually be separate, but nearby, to the main queue line.

Here, simply show your Front of the Line Pass to the Team Member. Typically waits will be 10 minutes or less for rides even on the busiest days – often they will be much less.

As you will be in a different queue line to the main one, FOTL Pass guests may lose some of the storyline told in the queue. Each member of your party will also need their own FOTL Pass.

Do I *need* a Front of the Line Pass?

If you are prepared to get to the theme park before it opens, it is achievable to see all shows and do all the rides in the park without a FOTL pass during regular park operating hours. If, however, you plan to visit during a busy period (e.g. Christmas, Spring Break, Summer) or if you cannot be at the park entrance just before opening time, a FOTL pass may be worth the extra cost for a hassle free visit with no waits.

VIP Tour Experience

The VIP Experience is a step up from the FOTL pass and the ultimate way to experience Universal Studios Hollywood, including several experiences that are unique to this tour.

It is a full-day service beginning from before you even step foot in the park, with valet parking and park admission included. You even have you own exclusive theme park entrance. Once inside the park, it's time for a continental breakfast in the private VIP lounge. Throughout the day, you will be escorted to the Front of the Line at Universal's most popular shows and attractions, and have lunch in the private VIP dining room. After your tour, you get unlimited FOTL access to all the rides on your own. You will be in a small group with other people who have also purchased the VIP experience.

Movie fans will love the private Studio Tour, with a small tram just for your group. You will even be able to step off the tram and roam some of the sets, enter soundstages, tour the audio department, and enter the movie studio's largest prop warehouse.

Pricing starts at $359 per person; children under 5 years old may not take part in this experience.

In addition, if you would like to reserve a VIP tour just for your family or group, this can be arranged with a private VIP tour.

Is the VIP Experience worth it?
Movie fans with some spare cash to spend will love this tour, especially with all the extra exclusive backstage experiences. If you are not interested in the extra features as part of the studio tour, you may be best off with a standard FOTL pass and saving the extra money. If money is no object, this is hands down the best way to experience the park and the best premium studio experience in Hollywood.

Single Rider

One of the best ways to significantly reduce your time waiting in queue lines is to use the Single Rider line instead of the regular queue line. This is a completely separate queue that is used to fill free spaces on ride vehicles. For example, if a ride vehicle can seat 8 people and a group of 4 turns up, and then a group of 3 takes the other seats, then a 'Single Rider' will fill the empty space on the ride vehicle.

The Single Rider queue ultimately makes the wait times shorter for everyone in the park as all spaces on ride vehicles are filled. Single Riders typically get on much more quickly, and the regular line moves marginally quicker as all those single riders aren't in it!

If the parks do get extremely busy then Single Rider lines can be closed. This happens when the wait in the Single Rider line is the same or greater than the regular line, thereby undermining its purpose. If the queue line is full and cannot accommodate more guests, it will also be temporarily closed. If the park is almost empty, then sometimes these lines do not operate either, as there is no need for them.

If you are travelling as part of a group, you can still use the Single Rider queue line – just be aware that you will ride separately, but you can still meet each other at the exit once the ride is over.

Single Rider lines are available on: *Harry Potter and the Forbidden Journey, Jurassic Park River Adventure, Transformers: The Ride, and Revenge of the Mummy.*

Child Switch

When two adults visit Universal Studios Hollywood with a kid who does not or cannot ride, there could be a problem if they wanted to ride a thrill ride – each adult would need to queue separately, as the other waits with the child, they would then swap. This would mean that they would wait twice for each attraction. However, at USH the solution is Child Switch.

Simply go up to a Team Member at a participating attraction entrance and ask to use Child Switch. Each ride works a little differently, but generally one or more adults will go in the standard queue line while another adult is directed to a child swap waiting area.

Once the first group has queued up and then ridden the attraction, they proceed to the Child Switch area. Here the first group will stay with the child, and the person who originally sat with the child gets to ride straight away, without having to wait in the queue line again.

This procedure may vary from attraction to attraction – make sure you ask the Universal Team Member at each attraction entrance about the procedure.

Child Switch is available at *Harry Potter and the Forbidden Journey*, *Despicable Me: Minion Mayhem*, *Revenge of the Mummy*, *Jurassic Park: The Ride*, *Transformers: The Ride – 3D*, and *The Simpsons Ride*.

Internet Access

Internet access has become indispensable over the past few years – whether you need to send a business email, look up the route to your next destination, check your credit card bill or upload a photo to Instagram.

You can find free Wi-Fi access throughout the theme park; the network is called "UNIVERSAL". The theme park also has a handy mobile website (**www.ushwaittimes.com**) that allows you to see attraction wait times in real time, as well as show and character schedules.

Stroller and Wheelchair Rental

USH offers stroller, wheelchair and motorized ECV rentals. The rental area is located to the right hand side after the theme park turnstiles.

You can rent the following:
* Single Stroller – $15 per day
* Double Stroller – $25 per day
* Wheelchairs – $15 per day, plus a $25 deposit.
* ECVs – $50 per day, plus a $25 deposit.

ECVs must be operated by a single person aged 18 years old or over. Wheelchairs can also be rented at CityWalk. Strollers must be folded before using the StarWay between Upper and Lower lots.

Chapter 9

Guests with disabilities

Visiting a theme park can be a complicated process for someone with a disability, but Universal Studios Hollywood has worked hard to give people in this situation as much of the full theme park experience as they can. Although, we could not possibly cover every kind of disability in this section, we have tried to include as much information as possible.

Universal Guest Assistance Pass

A Universal Guest Assistance Pass can really ease the day for some visitors. In order to obtain it you will need to go to Guest Services (to the right through the turnstiles) and ask for the Guest Assistance Pass.

Although it is not required, we strongly recommend you get a note from your doctor (in English) explaining what exactly you need help with - whether it is not waiting in the sun or not waiting for prolonged periods of time standing up or not waiting in crowded areas. It all depends on your situation. Your doctor does NOT need to explain your disability, just what help you require.

The Universal Team Members at Guest Services will ask you questions to determine eligibility and what type of help you need. As mentioned before, a letter from a doctor is not required but will greatly assist this process. You will be issued an Guest Assistance Pass and it will be explained.

Using the pass:
When you reach an attraction you would like to ride, show your Guest Assistance Pass to the Team Member at the ride entrance (the 'greeter'). If the regular attraction wait time is less than 30 minutes, then you will be immediately directed towards an alternative queue.

If the regular wait time for the attraction is 30 minutes or more, then the greeter will write down a time on your Pass to return – we will call this a 'reservation' for the purpose of this guide. This time will be the current time, plus the attraction queue length, Eg. It is 1:00pm and there is a 35-minute wait, so your return time will be for 1:35pm.

When that time comes around, show your pass with the reservation time at the ride entrance and you will be allowed entry through the alternative queue. This is NOT a front-of-the-line ticket and waits can still be up to 15 minutes. You can hold one 'reservation' at once, though you may enjoy faster entry to rides with less than a 30-minute wait, even if you have an active reservation.

If you want to change the attraction you have a reservation for, simply go to the next attraction and make a reservation with the attraction's greeter at the entrance. This will void your previous reservation.

Other accommodations for disabled guests

Deaf/Hard of Hearing – For guests who are deaf or hard of hearing, many in-park shows have signed performances. These can be reserved at no charge with at least one week's notice by contacting Guest Relations at 1-800-UNIVERSAL or e-mailing **guest.communications@nbcuni.com**.

Assistive listening devices for the hearing impaired are provided at Guest Relations free of charge. Amplified handsets are at all phone locations.

Mobility Impairment and Wheelchairs – Universal Studios Hollywood has been designed to be as wheelchair-accessible as possible. All shopping and dining facilities are accessible. Guests who would like to use a stroller as a wheelchair should ask for a special tag from Guest Relations.

Stage shows also have designated areas for wheelchair users and their parties. Most rides are accessible – some will require a transfer; others will allow you to ride in your wheelchair. Guests must transfer to a wheelchair in queues.

Note that you do not NEED to have a Guest Assistance Pass if you are in a wheelchair as all rides have an accessible entrance, but it can make things easier when there are particularly long queues, so we do recommend it. If you, or someone you are with, suffers from a disability that is not easily seen we thoroughly recommend the use of one of the Assistance Passes – without one you will need to use the regular queue line.

Service Animals are permitted throughout the theme parks but each attraction will have a specific way of boarding. The greeters at the entrance of each attraction will be able to provide more information.

Rides and shows:
Special restrictions apply to guests with prosthetic limbs and guests with oxygen tanks. More information about rides and shows specifically is available through the Riders Guide for Rider Safety & Guests with Disabilities (PDF file). It can be downloaded online from **www.universalstudioshollywood.com/site-content/uploads/2016/03/Riders_Guide_March-2016.pdf**. Printed copies are also available at Guest Services.

Chapter 10

Dining

When visiting Universal Studios Hollywood you will find an abundance of food choices, from standard theme park fare to Table Service dining, as well as snack carts.

Theme park fast food is generally priced at about twice what you would pay outside the parks. A $4 hamburger becomes $7-$8, and a drink will be about $3. A full meal will cost you between $14 and $24 depending on what options you choose.

Dining reservations

It should be noted that in the theme parks there are no Table Service dining locations, but only Quick Service eateries. Table Service locations are available just outside the theme park gates in CityWalk. As such, there are no reservations for any in-park restaurants. If you wish to make reservations for CityWalk, try OpenTable.com for some locations. Otherwise, you should call the restaurants directly as each is operated independently and there is no centralized booking system.

With the exception of peak dates, you should be able to get a reservation for most restaurants a week or so in advance. If there is a specific place you want to eat, we recommend you book your table as early as possible. However, we have frequently decided that we would like to eat a particular location and have known to get reservations on the very same day.

Top 5 Table Service restaurants at Universal Studios Hollywood

Universal has many Table Service restaurants dotted throughout *CityWalk*, so finding the best one can be a bit of a task. Luckily, we have rounded up those that you really should not miss out on below. Note that prices and menus change all the time with seasons and chefs – those that we have listed were correct as of when we ate at the locations and should merely be taken as examples.

1. Saddle Ranch Chop House – This Western-themed restaurant provides a laid-back environment to dine in, large portions, attentive service and even a mechanical bull in the center. There are also three full service bars in case you want to drink the night away after your meal.

---

2. Samba Brazilian Steakhouse & Lounge – Gourmet Brazilian cuisine done at its best served family-style on skewers. There are even all-you-can-eat options for those wanting to fill up ($35 at lunch and $50 at dinner). The cocktails here are not to be missed.

3. Buca di Beppo – Top quality Italian food, served in huge portion sizes and with friendly service. Dishes are served family-style to share meaning that prices are reasonable per person. Large pasta dishes for 3 to 5 people are typically about $39, for example. There is a decent wine selection too.

4. Camacho's Cantina – With authentic Mexican food and atmosphere, Camacho's is a vibrant place to dine. Burritos and enchiladas are $10 to $12, with fajitas in the $16 to $25 price bracket.

5. Tony Roma's – Yes, Tony's is a chain, but it can't be missed for the best baby back ribs. The steaks here are equally delicious, and there are many other dishes available. Portions are generous.

Top 5 Quick Service restaurants at Universal Studios Hollywood

Sometimes you do not necessarily want to sit down and have a three-course meal. You may want to use that time to watch a show, walk around the parks or ride your favorite attraction again – but that does not mean you want to compromise on taste. Here are our favorite on-site Quick Service restaurants. Note that prices and entrees change often; those listed were correct as of the last time we ate at the locations and should be taken as examples.

1. Three Broomsticks – Everything about this restaurant puts it top of the pile of quick service locations: the atmosphere, the food and its opening hours. Three Broomsticks is open for all three meals: breakfast, lunch and dinner, and is the only restaurant inside The Wizarding World of Harry Potter. Entrees are priced between $8 and $15. Breakfast entrees include breakfasts from around the world. Lunch and dinner fare revolves around British dishes with some American classics available too. You will find Cornish pasties, fish & chips, shepherd's pie, as well as smoked turkey legs, rotisserie smoked chicken and spareribs.

2. Krusty Burger – If you want the slimiest of burgers, then this is the place to go. Designed to be exactly as "artery-clogging" as the burgers are in 'The Simpsons' cartoons, Krusty Burger will not win any awards for being exotic but this location has hands down *the* best-tasting burgers at Universal. Entrees are priced between $8 and $13 with fries included. As well as burgers, you will find barbecue rib sandwiches and hot dogs. The burgers are, however, an acquired taste – many people we have spoken to didn't like the taste of the meat.

3. Gru's Lab Café – Themed around Despicable Me, there is a variety of choice here making it a good place to go for all tastes. From pulled pork sandwiches to tasty rotisserie chicken, every entrée we have had here has been a solid choice. For those looking for some Asian cuisine try Dr. Nefario's Lab Salad. Plus, try the desserts to round off your meal. They are incredible!

4. Jurassic Café – This is the best place to eat on the Lower Lot, in our opinion, serving mainly American favorites. The selection includes fresh salads, turkey legs, roasted chicken, personal pizzas and gourmet burgers. It is not hugely adventurous but there is a good chance you will find something here for most people, especially kids.

5. Plaza Grill – Lastly, this location gets a mention for serving breakfast until 11:00am, which can be hard to find inside the park. For the rest of the day, you will find sandwiches, burgers, turkey legs and other American classics.

Chapter 11

Tips, Savings and More
Money saving tips

Bring food from home – Universal allows you to bring your own food into the parks, so why not do exactly that? Whether it is a bag of chocolates or a drink, you can purchase these items at a fraction of the price anywhere outside of Universal property. For drinks, why not put them in a cooling bag (hard-sided coolers are not allowed in the parks), and/or freeze them to drink throughout the day. Food should be fine in a backpack throughout the day. Glass containers and bottles are not permitted in the parks.

Buy tickets in advance – Whatever you do, do not buy tickets at the gate – you will waste time and pay more than you need to. As you are reading this guide, we can safely assume that you will be doing some planning before you go, so there is no excuse not to buy your tickets in advance. You can do this over the phone, online at **www.universalstudioshollywood.com** or through a third party. You will save money on tickets by not purchasing them at the gate. What's more, if you purchase these tickets through the official Universal website, you will get one hour's early park admission to experience *The Wizarding World of Harry Potter* before other guests.

You do not NEED a Front of the Line Pass – By following our touring plan, you can see all attractions in one day. Save yourself over $100 per person by following our guide. If you want to do everything in half a day or want to arrive after parking opening, Front of the Line Passes are recommended.

Stay off-site – If you do not want to pay the high prices to stay at the few on-site hotels, then stay off-site. There are many hotels that are only just off Universal Studios Hollywood property – a two to three-minute drive away, or a 15-minute walk. Or with the convenient Metro subway system, you can get a hotel room slightly further away for a better price. These rooms can cost a fraction of the price of the on-site hotels.

Character photos – When getting your photo taken with a character, ask the photographer to take one with your camera too. Free photos instead of the park's exorbitant prices.

Free lockers – Universal charges for lockers at *Jurassic Park* but not at *Revenge of the Mummy*. Would they know for example if you put your belongings in another ride's lockers that are free and then walked over to the water ride? Absolutely not. It is up to you to decide if you use this trick or not as it does involve walking back and forth.

How to watch TV tapings for free

We have spoken a lot about Universal Studios Hollywood as a theme park, but as you also know it is a real working production studio. Therefore, you might be wondering how you can see one of these tapings in progress. The way to do this has nothing to do with the theme park. TV tapings are free to attend and the best place to check whether any tickets are available is at **www.tvtickets.com** - this lists tickets to many studios in the Los Angeles area, not only to Universal. Best of all, it is completely free to be in the audience!

When is the best time to visit?

Universal Studios Hollywood is open 365 days a year, so no matter when you visit you can expect the theme park, and its rides, to be open. The theme park has quite a few thrill attractions that appeal to the teenage market, as well as to families. As such, the majority of these visitors come to the park at the same time – doing school breaks.

Therefore, the busiest times of the year for the them park are: Christmas break, Halloween (for Halloween Horror Nights), Spring Break/Easter break and the Summer break. If you can visit outside of these times, you will find a much less crowded park.

A less crowded park makes for a much more pleasant experience, but you should also expect shorter operating hours out of season. Whereas the theme park may be open until 10:00pm in June, it will close at 5:00pm off-season.

You should also consider the weather for when you are touring. Los Angeles is famed for its sunny days but the weather can be unpredictable. The coldest months (late December to March) have average lows of about 50 Fahrenheit and highs of just under 70. The warmest months are July to September, with average lows of about 65 Fahrenheit and highs of about 85. Rain is extremely rare during the summer months. These temperatures can vary, of course, but give you a general indication. If you can choose any time of the year to visit, we recommend during Spring (April to June) or Fall (October to December) – and of course avoiding the school breaks as mentioned above.

How to spend less time queuing

Park opening – Make sure you get to the theme park well before it officially opens. Ideally, you should be at the entrance 30 minutes or more before opening. Remember it will take some time to park your car and get to the theme parks too. Early morning is the quietest time of the day, and in the first hour you can usually do three or four of the biggest rides, something that would take several hours later on. The park often opens earlier than advertised too, particularly during busy periods.

Use the Single Rider lines – If you do not mind riding separately from the rest of your party, take advantage of the Single Rider lines. See our section dedicated to these. They will reduce your time in queue lines significantly, meaning you can experience more things per day; they are available at a surprisingly large number of major attractions.

Touring Plan – We have expertly crafted a touring plan that tells you what order to do the attractions in; this has been devised to let you see as much as possible while spending as little time as possible in queues. Use it.

The 59-minute rule – If Universal closes the park at 5:00pm, that is when the queue lines (not the rides) will be closed. Anyone in the queue line at park closing time will be allowed to ride, no matter how long the wait is. This means that if you have one final ride to do and it is getting to park closing time, make sure that you are in queue line before the park closes to be able to ride.

This rule may not apply if an attraction has an exceptionally long line that would cause it to keep running for hours after park closing. This may be the case with *Harry Potter and the Forbidden Journey* on peak days.

Remember: The last Studio Tour leaves well before the park closes (usually 1 hour 40 minutes before).

Early Park Admission

How do you fancy being able to get into the theme parks before other guests? Benefit from much shorter queue lines at select attractions, and an emptier park, with Universal's Early Park Admission (EPA).

During most of the year, Universal Studios Hollywood offers one-hour early entry to *The Wizarding World of Harry Potter*. This benefit is available to guests who purchase park tickets directly on the USH website at **www.universalstudioshollywood.com** and also for guests who purchase a Universal Vacation Package including park tickets and a Preferred Hotel.

As *The Wizarding World of Harry Potter* is by far the most popular part of the park, being able to access it early in the day ensures lower wait times – a very valuable benefit.

Entry is one hour before regular park opening – meaning early entry is allowed from 8:00am most of the year (with the parks opening for regular guests at 9:00am), and 7:00am during peak season.

Operating Hours and Ride Closures

Universal Studios Hollywood is open 365 days a year and operating hours of the parks vary according to demand. On days when there are expected to be a lot of visitors, the parks are open longer, and when there aren't so many, the parks close earlier. The parks will always operate for their advertised operating hours. We strongly advise that you check these in advance of your visit. They may change closer to the date of your visit, so do re-check again.

Park operating hours can be verified many months in advance at **www.universalstudioshollywood.com/calendar**.

Ride refurbishments also happen throughout the year in order to keep rides operating safely and efficiently. As Universal is open 365 days a year, it does not close for several weeks or months at a time to refurbish rides like some other theme parks. Therefore, rides and attractions must close throughout the year in order to be renewed. Refurbishments tend to avoid the busier times of the year. Jurassic Park: The Ride is regularly closed during the winter months (January to March). The refurbishment schedule is posted at the bottom of the calendar page on the USH website.

Remember, as well as planned refurbishments, rides may close for technical issues or weather-related reasons. This is for your safety, and the engineers will do everything possible to get the ride back up as quickly as possible. There is no need to be angry at the ride attendants, as they have no control over whether the ride runs or not.

Ride Height Requirements

Many attractions at Universal Studios Hollywood have height requirements meaning that not everyone in your party may be able to enjoy every attraction. Height requirements are put in place for the safety of all guests to ensure they fit in the ride vehicles correctly. You will need to be measured at the entrance to each ride by a ride operator if you are close to the height limit – their word is final.

This section helpfully lists all attractions (except those without height requirements) in ascending order of height.

- **Flight of the Hippogriff** – 39 inches (0.99m)
- **Despicable Me: Minion Mayhem** – 40 inches (1.02m)
- **TRANSFORMERS: The Ride-3D** – 40 inches (1.02m)
- **The Simpsons Ride** – 40 inches (1.02m)
- **Jurassic Park: The Ride** – 42 inches (1.07m)
- **Revenge of the Mummy** – 48 inches (1.22m)
- **Harry Potter and the Forbidden Journey** – 48 inches (1.22m)

Chapter 12

Comparing Universal Studios Hollywood and the Disneyland Resort

Universal Studios Hollywood cannot be studied in a vacuum as it is not the only theme park in the L.A. area. Far from it; if it were not for the other big competitor in the district, Universal most likely would not even have built a theme park in California. We are of course referring to the Disneyland Resort: home to the first true *theme* park – and the second most visited theme park resort in the world.

The two resorts – Universal Studios Hollywood and the Disneyland Resort – can be compared. There are many similarities and many differences, so if you have visited one and not the other, this section should be able to provide you with an insight into what to expect. We hope this will help you be more prepared for your Universal Studios Hollywood experience.

Resort size – Universal Studios Hollywood, including CityWalk, the theme park and the entire studio filming area measures in at roughly 350 acres. However, if you exclude the Studio Tour, the actual theme park is a mere 40 acres in size.

In comparison, the Disneyland Resort measures in at about 440 acres. Disneyland Park is 84 acres in size (double the size of Universal Studios) and a second theme park, Disney's California Adventure, measures in at 67 acres.

The Disneyland Resort therefore boasts two theme parks, three on-site hotels and a shopping and entertainment district, Downtown Disney. Universal Studios Hollywood has one theme park (albeit with a huge Studio Tour), CityWalk for shopping and entertainment, and a couple of on-site hotels not managed by Universal.

Planning – A vacation to Disneyland requires a bit more planning because it is a multi-day destination. You will need to decide between one-park or two-park tickets, the length of stay and you need a strategy to make the most out of your visit and avoid huge queue lines. You need to understand the Fastpass system to make the most of waiting in lines, get to shows well in advance and know which rides to hit when. Plus, you should plan for fireworks and parades and how you will integrate these into your day. There are over 80 attractions to choose from, so chances are you will have to pick and choose between them.

Universal Studios Hollywood's big advantage is the fact it is so small. There is only one theme park, there are only a very limited number of attractions and therefore planning is much simpler. There is no need to reserve a restaurant in the park, as no in-park restaurants take reservations, there is no equivalent of a Fastpass system (you have either bought Front of the Line access or you haven't), ticketing options are simpler, and shows and rides are easier to get to. You should have a strategy for the rides (see our Touring Plan for a perfect example of this), but as there are fewer than 15 attractions, you can do them all in one day with a bit of planning.

Off-Season – We all know that visiting the theme parks during school breaks means that they are going to be busy; the kids are out of school and parents want them to have fun so the theme parks are naturally going to be filled with guests. What about out of season? Like September during school time, or February.

At the Disneyland Resort, you can expect to find crowds year round. There are quieter days than others, but there is never going to be a day at the Disneyland Resort that you can stroll onto Radiator Springs Racers within 5 minutes; it is never going to happen. Disneyland also has a huge number of annual Passholders who visit very, very frequently; the resort even had to suspend sales of certain passes in 2014 as crowds were becoming too big.

This is different at Universal; there are still lots of times of the year in off-season when almost every ride is a walk-on – these are times when you can experience *Harry Potter and the Forbidden Journey* in a matter or minutes instead of an hour or two! The off-season still exists at Universal. This has a lot to do with the target demographic of Universal with older teens likely being in school longer, whereas very young kids can visit Disney year-round. Annual Passholders at Universal are likely to visit less often as there are fewer things to do.

To compare, Universal Studios Hollywood had just under 7 million visitors in 2014, though we expect this to rise from 2016 onwards with the opening of *Harry Potter*. The Disneyland Resort in comparison saw just under 9 million visitors at Disney's California Adventure, but almost 17 million at Disneyland Park.

Having said this, if Universal continues to soar in popularity as it has done in recent years, it is very possible that the same 'lack of off-season' situation will develop, particularly as the parks have a very limited number of attractions.

Character meet and greets – At the Disneyland Resort, you have to plan which characters you want to meet and when, even with the possibility of making Fastpass reservations. At Universal Studios Hollywood, its more spontaneous and you should never have to wait more than 5 or 10 minutes to meet a character. Compare that to a 45-minute wait for the princesses at Disney and you can see the difference.

Hotel accommodation – Universal Studios Hollywood does not run any hotels itself but there are two on-site hotels run by major hotel chains. It is a short walk from both of these to the park or a shuttle bus is available. There is no extra Universal theming to these hotels, and you only get Early Park Admission if you book with Universal Vacations. The hotels and the theme park are very much two separate entities and the staff at the hotel are not knowledgeable as to the theme parks. Many hotels are available in the surrounding area.

In contrast, the Disneyland Resort has three on-site hotels owned and operated by Disneyland. These offer extra benefits such as package delivery, Extra Magic Hours (Early Park Admission), a food credit scheme, the ability to charge purchases in the theme park to your room key, and staff who are knowledgeable about the parks. There is no need for shuttle buses from the on-site Disney hotels as they are all within walking distance. Disney's Grand Californian Hotel offers exceptional theming and even a private entrance to one of the theme parks. These are just some of the advantages of everything being run by the same company. In addition, there are hundreds of non-official and partner hotel options just as close to Disneyland as some of the official hotels.

Attractions and theming – Disney is known for the nostalgia of its rides, with some having stuck around since opening day, over 60 years ago. You can still ride classics such as Peter Pan's Flight, though advancements have been made as Walt Disney always wanted his park to "never be complete" and to "keep moving forward". You can now meet the newest Marvel superheroes, hop on a flight around the world in Soarin' and get some high-speed thrills at Radiator Springs Racers. Disney appeals to everyone of every age, but with a stronger focus on family adventures. The theming at Disney's parks is second to none, with environments that immerse you in every direction you look. The construction of a Star Wars land will only add to this.

In contrast, Universal Studios Hollywood is definitely seen as more of an adult park. A good number of the attractions have minimum height limits, there are just two small play areas for kids and many of Universal's rides are reasonably intense and generally more thrilling than at Disney. Plus, the edutainment side of the Studio Tour won't keep kids amused. Theming in the park is few and far between and despite the effort to theme specific areas, it does feel odd how things change from one corner to the next. *The Wizarding World* of Harry Potter is one of the best themed environments in any theme park, but the visual intrusions from the park's other areas do ruin it a bit.

Lockers – Whereas at Disneyland you can take your belongings onto every single ride and keep them at your feet or in your pockets, at Universal Studios Hollywood, you must leave them in (free) lockers while you are riding a few of the attractions. This can be annoying, but admittedly it is safer for guests.

Friendliness – Although Universal Studios Hollywood helpful Team Members, their employees are nothing like Disney's. Disney's Cast Members are empowered to "make magical moments" to improve vacations in a way Universal employees cannot. Disney employees seem happier, and "courtesy" is one of 4 key company values.

At Disney's parks the only reason the courtesy of an employee could be compromised would be in a safety-critical situation. Otherwise, the Cast Members will go above and beyond, and provide exceptional customer service.

Universal Studios Hollywood, on the other hand, provides good service for the most part and most of the Team Members are great, but it seems that all too often during a visit these employees are overshadowed by those who are nonchalant at best, and rude at worst. Experiences vary, but Disney has the edge here.

Fastpass versus Front of the Line Pass – At the Disneyland Resort, your park ticket enables you to make free Fastpass reservations, which let you skip the regular queue lines by giving you a certain time to ride. These are made by visiting the Fastpass machines by each attraction you wish to ride, inserting your park ticket into the machine and taking it back, as well as your Fastpass ticket. Your Fastpass ticket will give you a 1-hour time slot to return and you can usually only hold one Fastpass reservation at a time. It is a bit of a complicated system to understand but guidebooks (like our very own *The Independent Guide to Disneyland 2016*) go through the whole process. The system only works on a select number of major attractions at the park.

The Front of the Line Pass at Universal allows you near-instant entry to every major attraction for a fee. This fee is in addition to your admission ticket and usually adds on at least $100 per person. You can only use your Front of the Line privileges once per attraction.

Leaving aside the fact that Disney's FastPass is obviously much better value as it is free, Universal's Express Pass (because of its paid nature) works better: there is rarely more than a 10-minute wait, you do not make reservations in advance, there is no complicated system to understand, less people use it and it is available for almost every single attraction. It is simple to use and useful.

Dining – Food at Universal Studios Hollywood is generally slightly cheaper than at the Disneyland Resort. However, there is nowhere near as much variety at Universal as there is at Disney; you will pretty much have to stick to standard theme park food at USH. The biggest difference in our opinion is the quality and taste; while food at the Disney's parks is not gourmet by any standard, in general, it is much better than Universal's.

There are also no Table Service restaurants inside the theme park at Universal, and the choice at CityWalk is limited. At Disney, character and Table Service meals are a big part of the experience, and the choice is larger.

Nightlife – As far as nightlife is concerned, Universal has a more adult feel than Disney. Universal has fully blown bars and clubs such as Howl at the Moon, whereas at Disney the closest thing you get to a nightclub is House of Blues. You will see many more families out at Disney, compared to Universal however and, generally speaking, Disney caters better for family-friendly activities than purely for adults.

Special events – Both Universal and Disney know that in order to keep people visiting all year-round, they need to offer seasonal events.

For Halloween, Universal offers a horror-filled portrayal of the season with *Halloween Horror Nights*, whereas Disney goes for a "not so scary" approach. Both theme park resorts offer after-hours paid events.

Christmas, however, is a much bigger deal at Disney than at Universal, with Disney hosting limited time shows, decorations, lighting ceremonies, nighttime spectaculars and more. Two attractions, Haunted Mansion and "it's a small world", even completely re-theme their interiors for this season. Universal holds its own Grinchmas event with a whole holiday season inspired by The Grinch with decorations, shows and character meets.

—
60

Chapter 13
Seasonal Events

Universal Studios Hollywood offers several seasonal events towards the end of the year. Whether it be horror mazes or Holiday cheer, the Universal team have it covered. This section covers the two main seasonal events each year.

Halloween Horror Nights
Select nights from mid-September to early November 2016
This is the biggest event of the year for Universal Studios Hollywood and takes place across both coasts – Hollywood and Orlando. It has been running for over 25 years.

Halloween Horror Nights is an evening extravaganza where there are heavily themed haunted houses, live entertainment and scare zones where "scarectors" roam around to frighten you. The theming is absolutely incredible at this event and unlike any other scare attraction in the US. As well as this, you will find most of the attractions open inside Universal Studios Hollywood.

As of the time of writing nothing has been announced for the 2016 events, including dates, theming or pricing. Information on the 2016 event should be released between July and the end of August 2016.

Halloween Horror Nights (HHN) is very, very popular and *Universal Studios Hollywood* does get extremely crowded during these events. Expect waits of 90 minutes or longer for each haunted house on most nights. This is one time when we highly recommend purchasing the *HHN Front of the Line Pass* if you want the full experience and to see everything, though it is an additional supplement that doubles the price of admission. You may need to make multiple visits to see everything on offer.

Dates:
Halloween Horror Nights runs on select nights from 7:00pm to 1:00am or 2:00am, depending on the day. Exact dates for 2016 have not yet been announced but the event generally runs from mid-September to early November 2016. The further your dates are from Halloween, the less crowded your visit is likely to be.

What is part of HHN?
Each year, the entertainment changes at Halloween Horror Nights, and this is one of the things that keeps people coming back again and again. For reference, in 2015 there were six different haunted houses – Crimson Peak, This Is The End 3D, The Walking Dead: Wolves not Far, Halloween: Michael Myers Comes Home, Insidious: Return to the Further, and Alien vs. Predator. Guests can expect the haunted houses to last about 3 to 5 minutes each. Haunted houses for 2016 have not yet been announced.

There were also four scare zones in 2015, where characters roam the zones causing fear; here you do not need to queue to be scared. In 2015, they were Exterminatorz, Dark Christmas, Corpz and The Purge. Also, scattered around the park are scare-actors with chainsaws...ready to run at you.

As far as live shows, 2015 was unusual as only one show was offered. This particular year it was a show by San Diego-based dance troupe Jabbawockees.

Finally, one of the highlights of the event every year is the Terror Tram – exclusive to this park. It is a short tram ride, followed by a walkthrough horror maze experience. In 2015, it was themed to The Purge.

Select attractions are also open during HHN. In 2015 these were: *Transformers, Revenge of the Mummy, Jurassic Park, The Simpsons Ride* and *Despicable Me.* Queues for attractions are generally non-existent throughout the event, as the focus is on the scare aspect of the night for most people. Guests with a Front of the Line Pass can use it for both the scare mazes and the attractions.

Universal warns the event "may be too intense for young children and is not recommended for children under the age of 13". Children under this age *may* enter as no proof of age is requested, but it is not recommended. No costumes or masks are allowed at the event.

Is The Wizarding World of Harry Potter part of HHN?
Information for the 2016 edition has not been released in regards to this – this is the first year that the *Wizarding World* has been in the park.

For reference, at Universal Orlando, the Harry Potter part of the park *is* open but with no additional horror theming– no scare-actors, no shows, no haunted houses. The area is open in its normal state. It is a safe refuge from the horror outside for anyone that needs a break. We do not know if Universal Studios Hollywood will follow the same model as the Orlando park.
Pricing:

Ticket sales for 2016 are not yet open at the time of writing. For reference, in 2015 a single **general admission ticket** was priced at $85 on the gate. Discounts of $5 to $26 are available at **www.halloweenhorrornights.com/halloween** in advance. We recommend you get your tickets in advance to save money; tickets sell out for popular dates.

Day + HHN combo ticket:
You can also add a night of Halloween Horror Nights to your daytime park ticket and save a substantial amount of money (versus purchasing them separately). The combo ticket saves you between $25 and $50 depending on the day of your visit.

HHN Front of the Line Passes:
Front of the Line Passes are available that combine a Halloween Horror Nights entry ticket plus unlimited expedited entry into each horror maze and attraction, as well as the Studio Tour and reserved seating at shows. Pricing generally starts at about $140. Front of the Line Passes do sell out in advance, so if you are considering one, get it early.

VIP Experience:
Although a VIP experience was not offered in 2015, it has been available in the past. The $220 VIP Experience includes VIP entry, unlimited front of the line access to all rides and mazes, valet parking, and access to the private VIP lounge with live music and food. It is unclear whether this option will return in 2016.

Halloween Horror Nights Top Tips:
- Although the event is listed as starting at 7:00pm, you can get early access to the park from 5:45pm to 6:15pm, with select mazes opening from 6:30pm.
- Costumes and masks are not allowed and you will be denied entry into the park. No food and drink may be brought from outside either. Security is very tight during HHN.
- The least busy days of the week are generally Thursdays and Sundays. Take a look at the pricing online: the cheaper it is, the less busy it is likely to be.
- Terror Tram closes before the rest of the park. See the park schedule.

Grinchmas
December

Unlike the Christmas season at Disneyland that runs from November, the Holiday season at Universal is much shorter. Dates vary each year but you can expect Grinchmas to run during select dates in December. Dates are not usually announced more than 2 weeks before the season starts, which makes planning for non-locals difficult. Grinchmas is included as part of your daytime admission and is not an extra charged event like Halloween Horror Nights.

For reference, in 2015, the event ran for 21 select days between December 5th and January 3rd. Dates for 2016 and usually announced only two to three weeks before the event starts.

As part of Grinchmas, you can expect:
- A tree-lighting show
- A meet and greet with The Grinch and Max (Grinch's dog)
- A meet and greet with Whoville Characters
- Martha May & The Who Dolls Dance Performance
- The Who-liday Singers Acapella Performance
- A 10-minute live show called "Story Time with Cindy Lou Who"
- The Whoville Post Office where postcards can be written
- "Trim Up the Tree Lot" where you can make your own tree ornaments
- Exclusive Grinchmas themed food on sale
- A short live performance from characters during the portion of the Studio Tour where you ride past set from Dr. Suess' "How the Grinch Stole Christmas".

As this is not your traditional Christmas season, there are no meets with Santa Claus at the park.

New Year's Eve

For the transition into the New Year, head over to *CityWalk* from 9:00pm and party the night away with live performances, a DJ dance party, lots of confetti and fireworks. The New Year's Eve party is a paid ticketed event, generally priced at $25 for adults and $15 for children. The event did not run in 2015, due to construction, but we expect it to return in 2016 but possibly in a modified format. Details are usually released in early December. The park itself does not celebrate New Year, as it usually closes before midnight.

Chapter 14

The Definitive Touring Plan

In order to make the most of your time at Universal Studios Hollywood, we highly recommend you follow our touring plan. This touring plan is *not* designed in order for you to have a leisurely, slow day through the parks, they are designed to get as much accomplished as possible, while still having fun.

This may mean crossing the park back and forth in order to save you from waiting in long queues, but ultimately it means you can get the most out of your Universal experience.

Our touring plan will have you riding the most popular attractions (those with the longest waits) at the start and end of the day when they are least busy; during the middle of the day you will be visiting the attractions that have consistent wait times, and watching shows. This enables you to maximize your time. Attractions are generally busiest between 11:00am and 4:00pm. Before 11:00am, people are still making their way to the park; after 4:00pm, most people have seen enough for the day. If the parks are open until late, you will find that most rides are 'walk-ons' in the last hour of park operation.

This touring plan presumes you do not have a Front of the Line Pass. If you do, then you can explore the park in whatever order you want, as you won't have to worry about waiting in the queue lines.

At the moment, Universal Studios Hollywood does not have an abundance of attractions meaning that wait times can be long throughout the park. It is, however, perfectly possible to do all the rides in the park on the same day with some planning.

The key to these touring plans is to arrive at the park well before it opens; that means being at the parking garages at least 60 minutes before park opening if you are driving in. The parking garages open at least 60 minutes before the park opens. If you want to buy tickets on the day, you will need to be at the park gates at least 45 minutes before opening. Otherwise, make sure to be at the park gates at least 30 minutes before opening with your park admission in hand. Park gates regularly open up to 30 minutes before the official stated opening time.

Using this touring plan: If there is a particular attraction you do not wish to experience, simply skip that step and then follow the next one - do not change the order of the steps.

One Day at Universal Studios

Due to the popularity of *The Wizarding World of Harry Potter* many people head straight to this area early in the day - DON'T! This is what everyone is doing, which means that you end up getting yourself into insanely long queues from the start of the day!

The exception to this is if you have Early Park Admission into *The Wizarding World of Harry Potter* – then you should, of course, explore all of this section of the park during this first hour, and then follow the touring plan below.

Step 1: Be at the park at least 30 minutes before opening. Remember that the park regularly opens before the official scheduled opening time.

Step 2: Pick up a park map and show times guide on the way in. These are usually available right by the turnstiles when entering.

Step 3: While everyone else is heading to *The Wizarding of Harry Potter* early in the day, we are going to make the most of our time by walking past Harry Potter towards *The Simpsons Ride* and then down the Star Way to the lower lot.

Step 4: Once on the lower lot, ride *Transformers*.

Step 5: This part of the park will still be practically empty. Ride *Revenge of the Mummy*. Feel free to re-ride if you want too. Sometimes this ride opens 30 minutes after park opening. If it is not yet open, follow step 6 first, then return to this step.

Step 6: If may be early in the day to get wet, but this is the best time to experience *Jurassic Park: The Ride* before the queues start to build up as it gets warmer. If you have followed this plan, you will have ridden three of the park's star attractions in under 45 minutes. These will get waits of at least 30-60 minutes each later in the day.

Step 7: Make your way back up to the Upper Lot and ride *The Simpsons Ride*.

Step 8: Ride *Despicable Me: Minion Mayhem*. This ride has constant long waits throughout the day.

Step 9: It is now time to ride the park's star attraction – the *Universal Studio Tour*. This will take about an hour in total to experience, plus the queue line. If you are feeling hungry, grab a snack to eat while waiting.

Step 10: Have lunch immediately after riding the *Universal Studio Tour*. The park will now be at its busiest with long waits for most attractions. We, however, have done almost every major attraction by now.

Step 11: After lunch you will be sitting through the park's major shows. Check their schedules and see them back to back. These include *Animal Actors*, the *Special Effects Show* and *WaterWorld*. You will usually need about two hours to see them all. If time is short, pick and choose – we would skip *Animal Actors* if we had to choose one not to see.

Step 12: Be sure to schedule in time to watch *Shrek 4D* as well. This is a show that seats a few hundred people every 15 to 20 minutes. The wait time sign for this show never goes below 20 minutes as that is how long it takes for a cycle of people to see the show. Therefore, if you see a 20-minute wait, chances are you will be in the next show. Note that there are higher than usual wait times for *Shrek* after each *WaterWorld* show finishes as many guests enter the queue for *Shrek* at once.

Step 13: If the new *Walking Dead* maze is open during your visit (opens summer 2016), go and experience this now.

Step 14: We are going to finish off the day with The Wizarding World of Harry Potter. Here, you have to play it somewhat by ear. *Ollivanders* and *Harry Potter and the Forbidden Journey* can both get some of the longest waits in the entire park. Do both of these attractions. If time is short, we would certainly prioritize *Forbidden Journey*. It is the best attraction in the park in our opinion. *Flight of the Hippogriff* may also be of interested to you – it is a small kids' rollercoaster. If you wish to watch any of the live shows in the *Wizarding World*, take a look at these too.

Chapter 15

The Future

The future of Universal Studios Hollywood looks bright and the park is currently going through a massive transformation. Several attractions closed to make way for *The Wizarding World of Harry Potter*, and many new brands have opened in CityWalk over the past few months breathing new air into this area of the resort.

The next major project being worked in for 2016 is a new year-round permanent horror maze. **The Walking Dead** will open in Summer 2016, replacing 'Universal's House of Monsters' that closed in 2015. The new maze will feature live actors, detailed sets and even animatronic figures. More details will be announced closer to the time.

There are rumors of *Revenge of the Mummy* possibly closing in 2017 to make way for a new attraction themed around The Secret Life of Pets or even Harry Potter. This has not been confirmed by Universal.

In September 2013, Universal's President and Chief Executive Officer, Steve Burke, announced at a conference that they plan to open one new attraction per year for the foreseeable future. This is a pace that no other major theme park resort can match, and sets an exciting precedent for the future.

Chapter 16

Park Map

Escalator to lower lot

Entrance

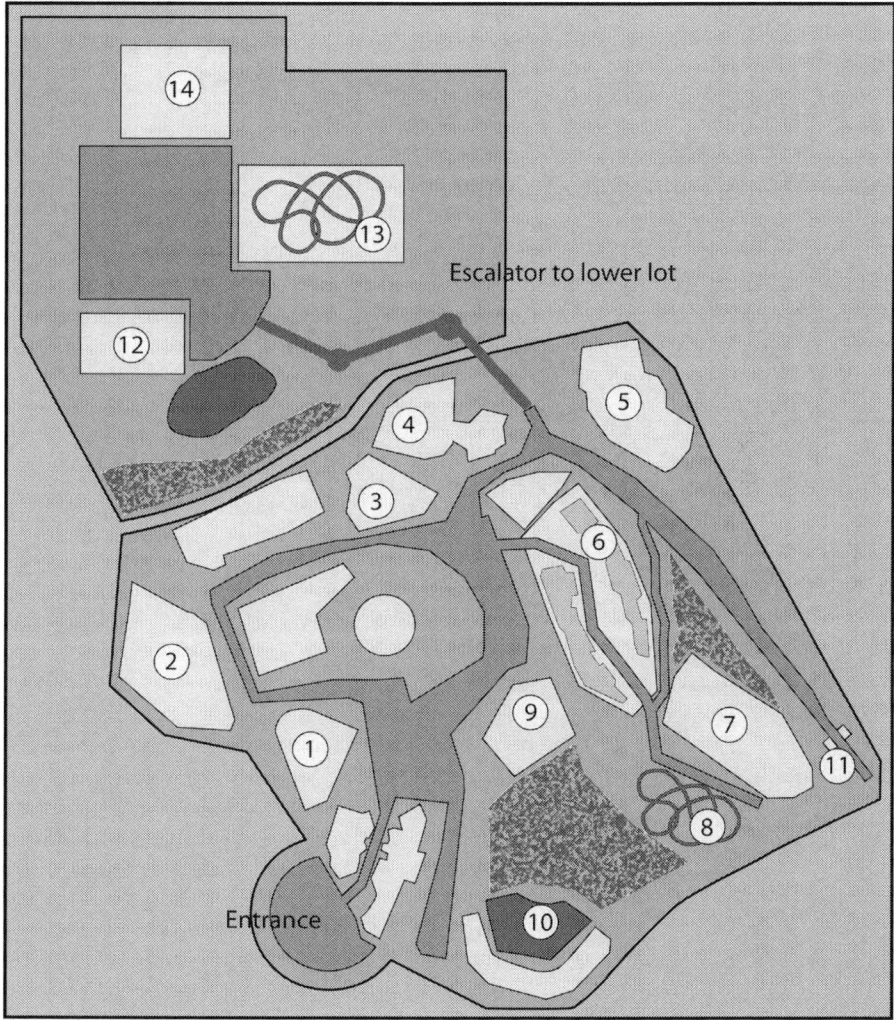

1 – Hollywood Globe Theatre
2 – Despicable Me: Minion Mayhem
3 – Universal's Animal Actors
4 – Special Effects Show
5 – The Simpsons Ride
6 – Ollivanders
7 – Harry Potter and the Forbidden Journey

8 – Flight of the Hippogriff
9 – Shrek 4D
10 – WaterWorld
11 – Universal Studio Tour
12 – Jurassic Park: The Ride
13 – Revenge of the Mummy
14 – Transformers: The Ride

Chapter 17

A Special Thanks

Thank you very much for reading *The Independent Guide to Universal Studios Hollywood 2016*. We hope this guide has made a big difference to your trip and you have found some tips that will save you time, money and hassle.

To get in touch, please use the 'Contact Us' form on our website at **www.independentguidebooks.com/contact-us/**.

Stay up to date on all the latest developments and updates by liking our Facebook page at **www.facebook.com/independentguidebooks** and following us on Twitter at **@indepguides**. You can also sign up to our newsletter on our website (on the right sidebar).

If you have enjoyed this guide you will want to check out:
The Independent Guide to Disneyland 2016
The Independent Guide to Universal Orlando 2016
The Independent Guide to Walt Disney World 2016
The Independent Guide to Disneyland Paris 2016
The Independent Guide to Paris 2016
The Independent Guide to New York City 2016
The Independent Guide to London 2016
The Independent Guide to Orlando 2015

Our theme park travel guides give you detailed information on every ride, show and attraction and more insider tips that will save you hours in line! Our city guides are great overviews of cities with top attractions, good places to eat and stay, explanations of the transport system and much more.

All that's left to say is: have fun at Universal Studios Hollywood!

Photo credits:
The following photos have been used in this guide under a Creative Commons attribution 2.0 license:

Universal globe (cover) – Miguel Discart; Tram (cover), and Jurassic Park Splashdown (cover) – Jeremy Thompson; Animal Actors and Waterworld (cover) – William Warby; Universal Globe (inside) – Prayitno; WaterWorld – Sebi Ryffel; The Simpsons Ride – distillated; CityWalk – Ana Paula Hirama;

Other photo credits: Loews Hollywood Hotel – thenewsfromeventworks.blogspot.com; Other hotel photos sourced directly from the hotels themselves. Some photos © Universal.

Made in the USA
San Bernardino, CA
08 October 2016